EMPOWERED
IN
Heels

Forward by Suzy Tamasy
Edited by Jennifer Traynor

WRITTEN BY

Susy Tamasy | Olimpia Tulpan | Cheryl Bailey
Demi Theo | Jennifer Traynor | Victoria Trinh
Sadia Salauddin | Kimberly Anne Cranley
Beverley Thomson | Mackenzie Lubeck
Sutha Shanmugarajah | Pat Kozyra

From the Pages of *Empowered in Heels*

"My father dismantled my mother's car so that she could not escape…my mom, sister, and I walked in the cold snow without shoes. We climbed the two hills to get to the closest neighbour and they didn't want to get involved."

Suzy Tamasy

"After eight years, three surgeries, and radiation treatments, my mother had lost her battle with cancer in August 2020. I felt like my heart had been pulled out of my body."

~ Olimpia Tulpan

"In the past, I had always put barriers up and played it safe. I feel ready now to stop saying no to myself and see where it takes me. With every "yes" I put out into the universe, more opportunities came my way."

~ Cheryl Bailey

"I can make something beautiful from what other people would see as garbage, but I see the potential and importance of everything."

~ Demi Theo

"My failures are like my battle scars, each one reminding me of how the lesson I learned from them made me stronger."

~ Jennifer Traynor

"I had watched all the family who put me down and continues to put me down all these years, be able to live their lives and I kept thinking to myself: when is it my turn?"

~ Victoria Trinh

"Who would have imagined that an awkward, insecure tomboy from Bangladesh would ever be a model? I certainly never did."

~ Sadia Salauddin

"I remember praying for a way out and praying to God saying, 'Please have a plan for me. Please don't let me go back to struggling to survive.' I think I prayed every day, all day in my head while crying."

~ Kimberly Anne Cranley

"Time has changed me, I'm stronger, I've walked through grief without prescriptions to numb the feelings."

~ Beverley Thomson

"One thing I would say about bullying is to not let it get the best of you. Always believe that you are amazing and strong, and never be afraid to stand up for yourself when someone has done you wrong."

~ Mackenzie Lubeck

"Over time, I placed my focus on things I wanted to do, and, in doing so, I gained self-confidence and independence. The thought of getting married and starting a family was far from my mind."

~ *Sutha Shanmugarajah*

"What these experiences have taught me is that while we may not always win at life, there are always other chances to excel and that even the disappointing moments can teach us valuable lessons."

~ *Pat Kozyra*

Empowered in Heels

"It's wonderful to see a group of women come together and share their stories and journey. A group that has been resilient and strong against so many challenges. Women that can encourage, inspire and lift others up. *Empowered in Heels* is just that." ~ ***Shelley Marsala***

"It takes a special person to overcome trauma, or to even distance themselves from it. It comes in various forms and they are all devastating in their own way. Reading about Suzy's journey is heartbreaking yet very inspiring. Her inner strength and spirit were challenged numerous times in several different ways, but deep down she always knew there was hope and something better on the other side. It's not always obvious or clear at the time, but believing is so important. Being able to turn it around and then make a mission out of serving others is the ultimate feeling of satisfaction, and Suzy has done just that and it's admirable.

I am very interested in reading this book to better understand the journey these women have lived through and overcame, and decided to share. It helps to see what others have been through, as it's a way of learning from experiences that you don't necessarily need to struggle through yourself. There are many stories out there of people that have lived through their traumatic experiences, and they need to be shared and normalized. Most importantly, to help free the victim of their past, but also to share with others so they know they aren't alone, especially for anyone currently in a situation they are unsure how to escape from. There is always hope, even when it feels there is none." ~ ***Michael AuCoin***

"I've known Suzy for almost ten years for her act of kindness and how she strongly supports the women's shelters (and how it) relates to her resilience and determination to change the cycle of abuse. I look forward to reading her story and other co-authors in *Empowered in Heels*. I know it will impact other women's lives and empower them with genuinely inspiring stories that make a difference." ~ *Arshad Awan*

"I have had the privilege to meet a couple of authors that are sharing their stories of hardships, trials, and abuse.

I hate words like "inspirational" at times because they've become so overdone, but I have to say these authors are truly an inspiration. I had the privilege of spending time in my home with Suzy Tamasy, and she is one of the warmest, funniest, smartest, down-to-earth people I have ever seen in this world.

Some of these stories are about women in relationships or married and struggling to maintain that marriage; about motherhood; about being thrown into terrifying decisions and positions. About finding the inner strength that they did not know existed.

There are moments of *exultation* and frustration, of pain and glory. Help celebrate with these authors as they share their successes and desire to help change lives.

Having suffered a terrible marriage and severe abuse myself, I was shattered and had to rebuild a life for myself and my children. Most victims do not know where to go or what to do.

This book is about life-changing journeys of tragedy and triumphs.

This book speaks of love, truth, and healing and I am excited to connect with the authors through their stores." ~ *Stacey Burns*

"This book had me in tears for all the right reasons. I hate words like, "inspiration" because they've become so overdone and cheesy, but I have to say it....

Suzy is an inspiration. Her story is about domestic abuse, about the fear and insecurities of living through it. It's about having the determination and the dignity to turn her life around, and that she did. Suzy's story is about believing in yourself and not giving up.

I don't think there's anyone who wouldn't benefit from reading her book. I know I did. " June-Marie Vieau

Table of Contents

Foreword

By Suzy Tamasy

This book is a dream and vision I had three years ago but have been putting it off since I didn't want my story to come to light. I don't want others to think of me as a victim. I did not share my story of trauma and things I have had to endure so others do not feel sympathy for me. I see my trauma and past as my strength to inspire and assist as many people as I cross paths with as a mission to make a difference in someone's life.

But the time has come to do it. I want this book to empower women out there. When you are experiencing the darkest days, feeling like you are drowning, I want you to know that there's always a light at the end of the tunnel.

I am truly blessed to be surrounded by a sisterhood of women who are part of my dream as co-authors in this book, all of whom have shared true inspirational stories of their lives and the feelings they also endured to make a difference.

When I sat and thought about what the factors of an inspiring story were, I found the answer in each one of the co-authors. Every woman in this book has a unique story to tell, all of which will touch your life and prompt you to want to make an impact by assisting others.

Empowering others is exactly what I wanted this book to do and my dreams are finally coming to fruition. The experience of putting this book together was so surreal to share with these amazing and inspiring women, as well as having an editor to share and brainstorm with. People ask me how I do it, and I just say that I do it with my heart and I know God leads me on the right path of where I need to be. I feel blessed to be connected with amazing people and it's true what they say – like attracts like, so if you think good thoughts, do good things, and practice positive habits, everything will just fall into place.

I was not always like this, though. I too struggled and had self-confidence issues. In the past, I never thought I was good enough. I always thought I didn't deserve to be treated well or to experience the best things in life. I completely lost myself. I've always wanted to give the best to my kids and not have them suffer as much as I did.

Despite past sufferings, I would never change anything I had to experience because it led me to be the woman I am now. I think our challenges make us stronger and if it wasn't for that, I wouldn't be where I am today, accomplishing goals every year with satisfaction. It has made me determined, resilient, and focused on what I deserve and want.

If there is one message that I would like to give to women out there, it's this: You deserve the best in life! You deserve to be treated with kindness and respect, to feel proud of who you are, and to attract all the best things life has to offer!

I have learned that internal beauty matters more than the external. If you have the beauty outside but do not have a good heart, then you are depriving yourself of magnifying the beauty of the whole. I have been blessed to work with so many beautiful physical aspects of people. If you start to analyze people you might see that most women who appear to be 100 percent perfect portray an emptiness inside. If you have beauty inside and out, you send out a vibration to others and they can see the confidence you carry that allows you to find the true meaning of happiness.

I asked myself, "Who am I, what do I want, and what do I want people to like about me?" I figured out why I love to dress up people as a stylist because I went through that time when I lost myself and didn't want to dress up or have a meaning in life.

I found my 'why' by dressing up and it uplifted my vibration from the start of my day. To allow great things to come to me naturally through the law of attraction. I am a keen believer in the law of attraction and know this has assisted me to be where I am today. It has helped me go through the darkest days when I fell into two abusive relationships and didn't understand why I deserved it.

I almost lost the condo I purchased in Toronto when my ex-husband took my overdrafts and left me with debt to punish me for leaving him. I had my two boys to take care of and didn't know how I would provide them with food, school money, and clothing, plus a roof over their heads. I hustled, did my full-time job, and worked hard on my own business.

I had faith in myself and transformed myself from feeling like I was nothing to owning my empowerment. I've never told anyone about the time I had my children's bags pre-packed and a planned emergency exit; how I had my ex-husband push through the door and unable to get him to leave. I had to call the police and have them remove him. He was given three days to go through the apartment to get his things and he ended up taking my passport, my children's passports, and other personal items as a way of having control over me.

He made it sound like I was crazy; that I was the reason for him to be provoked into a state of rage. I had to walk on eggshells to avoid him becoming a monster. I had to record our last interaction and play it over 20 times so that I could hear that it wasn't me who was the problem, it was him.

My sons and I were sitting at the table playing chess. My ex walked in and started throwing items at me, calling me names, saying that I was worthless and that I was a bad mother. I empowered myself by not being naive anymore and vulnerable to his apologies. He was to blame and it had finally sunk in.

I took ownership of my life and vowed to change. I reminded myself that I am worthy, good enough, and deserved better, as well as my kids. I did not want that cycle to continue; it had to stop!

I also have never shared about the time I called my mother, crying and telling her that he hit me again, to which she replied that I would not find a better father for my kids. I did not want to believe I had to live the life I grew up with and didn't want this for my boys.

I had to break that pattern and what helped me is to know I deserve the best in life. I felt like a woman in an inspirational movie who decides she will change her life for the better if it's the last thing she does!

All of this is why I have a personal mission to help other women out there be able to accomplish what I did. Today, I have a Ph.D. in physiology, and I'm a registered Hypno-cognitive behavioural therapist who has assisted over 5,000 women throughout my 20 years of entrepreneurship and dealing with several women shelters. I have supported women by assisting them to plan an emergency exit, helping them start from scratch, working with the court system to assist them, teaching them to build themselves up to having more and feeling empowered. I will continue to do what I love to do and will assist as many women as I cross paths with; this will be my effort to stop the cycle of abuse. I wish I had someone that would have empowered me on my journey, one of the reasons why I wanted to make this book possible – a source to motivate other women.

Each woman featured in this book has lived through different experiences, but what they all have in common is that they all have a story to tell, and we have used our stories to inspire others. I am so blessed to share our first book amongst these other empowered women!

We all have a story its what we do with our story that impacts others!

With Luv, Suzy Tamasy

Photo credit JT Taylor Women Expo Mississauga

14

MISSISSAUGA LADIES NIGHT

On February 7, the Sandman Signature Hotel played host to the annual Mississauga Ladies Night. There were exhibits featuring all the luxuries that gals love including apparel, jewelry, handbags, makeup, skincare products, spa services, health and fitness products, gourmet foods, designer items, and services for the home. There was a runway fashion show and on-stage product demonstrations. Spotlight specials and giveaways were offered throughout the evening and the first 75 people through the door received free swag bags. This feel good women's expo gave all who attended a chance to run wild during a fun evening of inspiration, education, and entertainment!

Event by Galen Carton
Website code: pewdwq5

Michelle, Event organizer Sarah & Bojana

The Fashion show models

Jia, Neelam, Shivani & Jyoti

Anderson, Sylwin & Laura

Audrey & Kaley

Create and Get Event Tickets at **northmississauga.snapd.com**

Featured in Media

15

Editor's Note

By Jennifer Traynor

When I was asked to be the editor for this book I was flooded with emotions. I was happy and excited to be finally doing something that I'd dreamed of doing for over 20 years, but I was also nervous to be taking on this project. While I have editing experience – I've edited articles, blogs, newsletters, and even a short e-book – this was my first time editing a book.

This was a project I put my heart and soul into. As one of the co-authors, I allowed myself to open up in a way I haven't before, and as the editor, I dove into the process with a positive mindset and with confidence. Yes, this was a challenge for me, but a good one, and one that I felt ready to add to my repertoire. During the process of editing this book, other opportunities arose for me to edit other books. Thus began my journey into book editing!

Having the privilege to go through each of these phenomenal stories and to have been entrusted with editing the heartfelt words of my co-authors was truly an honour. Believe me, these women have remarkable stories to share and when you finish reading this book you will be inspired, motivated, and uplifted. Each of us has faced hardships in our journeys, and our stories are all different, but what we all have in common is that we came through the other side stronger than before.

The main reason why I was so drawn to the opportunity to edit and co-author *Empowered in Heels* is that I wanted to be a part of something that I believe is going to make a difference to women out there. I truly believe each story will help other women see that they are not alone in their journey, that they can get through whatever they may struggle with and come out stronger, and that they are worthy of achieving amazing things!

Thank you, Suzy Tamasy, for believing in me and having the faith that I would get this job done well. I am so proud of what we have all accomplished with this book. Thank you to the amazing women, with whom I share these pages, for your vulnerability, and for having the courage to share your stories.

Finally, to our readers, thank you for going on this empowering journey with us.

Blissful Haze Photography

Inside My Jewellery Box

By Suzy Tamasy

You don't know it until you go through it, but you can survive and break any pattern. This is the story of how I did just that.

People ask me why I do what I do. I say to them that I do it with a full heart of passion! Through clothing pieces and jewels, I work to uplift the women that think they have no significance in life and inspire them to become the shining jewel that they deserve to be. This is why I do what I do with *SuzyQJewels*. As I've mentioned to others, it's not about the clothing, but rather, my passion for giving back to the women's shelters that drives me to do what I do. My work is the good that came out of the bad that I've experienced in my life.

Remembering my childhood always gives me a sense of pain, sadness, and a powerless feeling of failure. From what I thought I did not deserve to what I see today. I had to break through that pattern to allow myself to finally leave my past behind and empower myself by acknowledging that I do deserve the best in life. I believe our minds hold our full potential in life, but it's what we say to ourselves that hurt us the most and stops us from achieving more.

If anyone knew what I had to see and the story I had to make up to cover my father's beatings it would sadden you. I remember being four years old and having a black eye from my father, who would get abusive when he drank. I told my teacher that I fell because I was told to lie.

I remember the fierce anger I had, and how I hated liquor because it made my gentle father transform into a monster. I would have to hide my father's tools under my bed so he wouldn't find them. I would have to get between my mother to stop the beating and take the beatings myself to save my sister.

Please don't think he was a monster since it was the strong liquor that was the monster. I hated it to my core. When he was drinking, I remember thinking that if I had to defend my mother, I would hit him back due to that fierce anger that built up and my protective attitude. From the outside of our beautiful home, nobody knew what happened inside.

It was a roller coaster for us when we were young. For a couple of days, we had an amazing dad, and the rest of the week the part-time monster would appear and we couldn't sleep. We prayed he would fall asleep and the day would be over. Despite all of that, I truly loved him since my memories of the great dad without the alcohol were a quiet, hard-working man, always wanting to save money and trying to give us the best he knew.

How I loved it when he cooked with his passion for food! Due to his Hungarian background, he would make goulash, paprikash, cabbage rolls, and the amazing poppy seed strudel, which always made us so excited.

My father carried a lot of sadness and the feeling of isolation from his mother, which made him suffer from depression. This is why he took to the drinking to cover his pain. At least, that was my conclusion when I reflected on all of it after he died in 2009 of stomach cancer. It was so hard to see a handsome man deteriorate with so much pain and suffering.

My father suffered from rejection from his mother when she gave priority to his older brother in everything and he felt left out. From education to attention and the lack of love given to him. My father dreamed of becoming a dentist, but in Europe the situation was hard and they were frugal and struggled to survive.

I think this is where it started. His family couldn't afford to send two sons to university, so they sent his brother, who became an engineer, and my father went to technical school to become an electrician. He was very smart, but experienced trauma in his life.

When he was 18 years old, his brother suffered from depression and took his life. My father felt empty and his mother, who fell into a deep depression, told him that she would have preferred if he would have been the son that died. Imagine what it is like to hear those words from your mother.

Forgiveness is Key!

At times I loved my father and sometimes hated him, but I forgave him when he became ill in his final days. I prayed that he did not suffer anymore and that God would send him to heaven with forgiveness.

I still recall the last days of his suffering. My mother knew he drank away all his money but hoped he had some left to help us. Yet he still did not give out his bank number and left us with nothing. My father was a stable worker before he got together with friends that loved to drink, so gradually, he could not maintain work and continue to do his profession from my younger years. His drinking made us lose our house and cottage.

My mother was my superhero. I still do not understand why she stayed with a monster, but I owe my mother my life. She was our super mom *and* dad in our broken family, she worked so hard to maintain a roof over our heads. I know inside of her she suffered so much, yet at the same time, she was resilient in wanting to change my father. It is said that you cannot change a person if they do not want to, but my mother's perseverance and true love kept her thinking differently.

I loved my mother so much that I felt I had to grow up quickly to protect and be on guard for any explosive events that would occur with my father. I was like the sister she did not have here in Canada.

My mother grew up in Venezuela and was one of 14 children! My grandmother was a hard worker and she sold clothing and other items to make a living (I like to think I inherited her business savvy). She travelled constantly and had nannies to take care of her children. She was tough, so now I know where my mother got it from.

My grandmother didn't allow my mother to even walk with boys and was punished a few times when my grandmother found her missing from school or walking with a male friend.

One day, my mother walked home from school with a boy, whom I think if she stayed in Venezuela she would have married. My grandmother got so mad and sent my mom to

Trinidad to study. Imagine being sent alone to a country, not knowing how to speak English or know anyone there.

Zero English, Tough Love

My mother lived in Trinidad for three months and she started to slack off in school when she began to meet other people there. My mother always told us that was the best time in her life. My grandmother got so mad again, so she sent my mom to Canada, where she was placed with a roommate and went to school to learn English for four months. After that, she met my father. He was handsome and successful at the time. He drove a yellow Corvette and had a job so my mom thought her Prince Charming had arrived.

After I was born, he started to hang around with friends who drank and influenced him in a bad way to become more aggressive. My mother wanted to buy a house in the High Park area of Toronto. She truly loved that area and they almost bought the house, but it didn't happen. We still pass by to see it today.

Instead, my dad's friend told him to invest in property close to Muskoka Lakes. He bought a huge lot there that was isolated from everything and everyone.

It was our terror place with mostly bad memories, though some were good. We dreaded the days we had to drive four hours to the cottage. He built a five-bedroom cottage in the woods where no one lived except another cottage up two big hills. It became my father and his friend's place to party, and the beginning of all the losses we had.

I have so many stories from those days. One, in particular, was the time when my father dismantled my mother's car so that she could not escape, and how my mom, sister, and I walked in the cold snow without shoes.

We climbed the two hills to get to the closest neighbour and they didn't want to get involved. While I write this, tears stream down my face as I think of memories and live them again. I remember my mother bleeding, us being lost, and not knowing what we were going to do. We ended up sleeping in a cold car, freezing, and asking our mom what would happen. She just looked at us and cried, then left us in the car parked at our cottage and went inside to check if my dad fell asleep.

She told us to stay in the car and we waited for my father to fall asleep. We were scared and cold in the dark, waiting for our mother to return and let us know that we could go back to our rooms. We were worried and I did not want to stay in the car, but I had to for my sister. It was tough to think about what my dad could do to my mom.

Eventually, my mother sold the cottage and moved us all to Venezuela in the hopes that my father would change. My sister and I cried because we didn't want to go, and my parents decided to adopt a dog, whom that we fell in love with since we never were allowed to have pets except for a canary. Our dog was our confidant who saw everything. His name was Kishlane and he was the best thing that we can say made us complete.

When we flew to Venezuela, we cried on the plane, thinking about how we knew my father would not change. We worried about where we would live and did not know what to expect. Our life there taught me that we need to be grateful for simple things, like having a glass of safe water to drink. We learned that you do not need a lot to be happy.

This is one thing I truly love from my time in Venezuela. They live and enjoy life without all the stuff.

Being Grateful for What We Have is Important

My best times were in Venezuela when I worked as a model for a year with Elite Models Inc. It was an amazing time in my life that helped me feel empowered for the first time.

I learned Spanish within a year of being there since the schools do not allow you to get credits until you know the language fluently. I was also nominated to be the queen for a pageant and won the crown. I learned the significance of beauty and dressed the part. I took up scuba diving and became an instructor for the shallow areas in the gorgeous oceanfront for a well-known hotel. I truly loved everything about Venezuela except my personal home life with my father and I would avoid it with work and school.

Around the same time, I also fell in love. I was 17 years old and thought he was my Prince Charming until I realized he was not what I thought. Can you be in love at 17, or was I just trying to escape my father? My 'Prince' did not drink, but he was verbally abusive and controlling. Yet, I begged my mother to sign the papers permitting me to get married. He would tell me I was worthless and could not accomplish much. He wanted a mother figure to cook, clean, and stay home. I could not wear shorts or skirts, and even a bathing suit was a big issue. I started to lose myself in this relationship. Our marriage ended when he couldn't come to Canada. I truly was so disappointed in men and never wanted a relationship again.

I managed to take my sister out of living with my parents, and worked and went to school. We finally had peace and it felt so good. Eventually, I found myself again and continued my life with school and work. I graduated from college in Biotechnology and Applied Sciences, and then went on to work as a laboratory technologist. I always liked to challenge myself! At that time, there were six females in the chemical and biological fields. I knew I was different and didn't follow the female masses of career path choices. I still look at my graduation photos and admire the females who were in the field, making an impact on the education path, and opening doors to other females to get into unconventional career paths. It was a man's world but I managed to work in the industry for years and eventually got into the corporate finance industry.

Soon after, I met another person who was introduced to me. At first, I thought he was not the person that I wanted to be with but after a while, I fell for him. Things were great and I loved getting the care and love from him.

Unfortunately, I did not learn from my first love and found myself in another bad relationship. Still, I gave it a try since it was good in the beginning. When our first child was born there was a shift in his behaviour. He became controlling, obsessed, drank alcohol, and could not keep a stable job. I felt like I was walking on eggshells, unsure of when he would lose it and strike at me. He was irresponsible and I found myself taking on the weight of the world on my shoulders. I felt lost, empty and upset that I was suffering again with an abusive husband.

I had managed to fall into my mother's footsteps of covering up for my husband and taking the world on my shoulders. I continued making excuses for the father of my kids. Although he wasn't totally a bad father, he lacked in so many areas and it was the irrational behaviour that I had to let go of. I think he also had depression and mental health issues that weren't diagnosed until later in his life. I wondered why this was happening to me. Is it that I don't know what true love is? Do I deserve this?

Was it that I thought so low of myself, I had to continue in this cycle and not get out sooner? I left my children's father three times due to physical altercations, but the fourth time was an eye-opening experience because I found my son doing the same things to me as his father had done.

I had to stop to take a look at myself and decided that I can't continue this pattern for my kids; I didn't want them to follow this path to either become an abuser or a victim. This was my turning point in finding myself and the hardest part of stopping the pattern. I thought back to when I was a child and how I criticized my mother, wondering why she stayed with my father. Now, I found that I was doing the same. It was a true epiphany moment and I said "no more" to the unsettled life that mimicked my childhood and the shadow that I carried with me.

We often judge people on who they are and what they do, but if you don't know what they've had to endure, whether they overcame it, or had the support to do it, then who are we to judge? It's so crucial to have a mindset of determination, resilience, and to want to have a better life for your future and your children, and if you can push yourself to get there, you will!

This is why I believe it's so important to seek counselling for victims so that they don't become abusers and continue this vicious cycle. I didn't want my son's future to be one as an abuser. It is so important to get help and counselling for the mothers and children who come from domestic abuse, and having women's shelters open to doing this is a key need that *SuzyQJewels* continues to support.

Gratitude for Everything

I am thankful that God made me strong enough to manage to get out of the cycle and not to look back. My children both have peace and calm at home now. I am so grateful to overcome so many challenges which are not covered in this story, but I can say that this is why I'm passionate about assisting other women who have been abused to break the silence and get out safely.

Now, my eldest is 23 years old and understands that his dad had a problem. My son's father was diagnosed with bipolar disorder in 2017. I have had to battle in court to get child assistance and much more, and I have truly sacrificed myself for my children. They will always come first until the day I die. I love them so much and want to give them the life I always wanted to have.

Through the pandemic, I had to reflect on the *SuzyQJewels* charity and ways we can generate funds to continue to donate. We incorporated more tops and lounge attire to sell, as well as added our *Cognibeu* program, which is a monthly gathering currently held online as a support to other women who've fallen into the cycle of abuse.

We deep-dive into our conscious mind and pinpoint areas where we are vulnerable to analyze ways we can share, develop self-love, and grow our inner core. This is something you can achieve if you put your mind to it, but most of all, when you acknowledge that you deserve the best in life.

My message to others is to remember to love yourself and take care of yourself first. Make sure to get out of abusive cycles because it will not get better. They can promise you that they will never do it again, but it always repeats. It is so important to have a support system in place, and counselling can be key for you and your children to move on. Stay strong and know that you are loved.

Dedication

I dedicate my story to all the women out there who think they cannot do it alone or feel unworthy. I want them to know that they can accomplish what they put their mind to. Love yourself, find out who you truly are, and believe that you deserve the best in life. Stop taking the verbal and physical abuse because you deserve so much more for yourself and your children to stop the cycle of abuse. This story is to inspire you, support you, and empower you to take charge of your life.

I dedicate my life and story to my amazing children, Austyn and Krystian, I love you with all my life! You are the best thing that has happened to me. You keep me striving to assist as many people as I can.

I am truly blessed to make a difference with kindness and a good heart, not asking for anything in return, and to share my empathic heart and goodness. I hope I have instilled those qualities in you and hope you continue the legacy in the future. I cannot understand why I fell into an abusive relationship, but I know it made me stronger and would not change anything in my life.

I dedicate this story to my superwoman mother, who is my rock and the person I look up to most, as well as my sister, whom I love. Even though there have been differences, we still have the bond of a family and are always there for the good and the bad. To my loving daughter in law, you have been my blessing! To all the models, photographers and so many others in which would be a book of its own. Thank you, GOD I wouldn't be, where I am without you!

AS SEEN IN:

Fashion Week Dress designed By SQJ Below Photoshoot

Photoshoot with SQJ design photocredit BR

Photographer Bal Syan

My Loving Boys that I live for and that keep me going

Kate & Dru Wedding gown by SQJ

Model Chantel Curry wearing SQJ Designs Published photo taken by Arshad Awan

First Divas & Durham Biz & Fashion Magazine Launch

Photo credit Andrej Baca

Styled shoot in Milton

MODEL   SARA DIBERT CRYSTAL MCKAY
ALEXIA MAGNUSSON CHANTEL CURRY,
OCEAN PRATT, CLAUDITA HANNAH GARRAWAY
KRYSTIAN NEMO MARINE AKPALO DILPREET
NANDHAWA MUA HEENA MUA AND NICKY LACHINI

SHE IS ENOUGH

SAFERGIRL

38

Aesha Malik and her Dad coming out from Cambridge to Divas in
Durham receiving our CogniBeu award for our professional Counselling

Published in Marika with a Creative Concept Earth - Wind & Fire with Jewellery Designer KIB Photo credit Faisal Hafeez

I CHOOSE TO BE KIND BECAUSE IT MAKES ME HAPPY. BUT I WILL DEFEND MY BOUNDARIES AND MY LOVED ONES WITHOUT HESITATION. MAKE NO MISTAKE: I AM FIERCE.

~Miracle~

Today's Pain is Tomorrow's Power

By Olimpia Tulpan

Twenty years ago, I emigrated to Canada from Romania and it was the most amazing thing I have done. Since I was a kid, I dreamed of escaping the communist country I lived in and being able to live my life free. I love being in Canada! I now feel free and happy to be able to do what I want to do!

In 2012, I started my Feng Shui and decorating business after working within the construction industry for six years. Who would have thought a stylish fashionista and model would work in the construction industry? It just goes to show the determination and guts I had, to accomplish what I wanted, as well as to be able to stay in Canada to help my mother and family in Romania.

From there, I began investing in real estate, mainly purchasing and flipping condos. People couldn't understand why I was working for a construction company and also modelling at the same time, but the hard work has paid off.

It was difficult being in Canada with no family. I kept myself busy working to make my dreams come true, but in the early years of being here, I found myself getting depressed. Being alone led to unhealthy habits, like eating bad food and drinking with friends. As I realized that this is not good for my health, I started my journey to healthy living by hiring a trainer and nutritionist to help me get in better shape. I chose a complete life change to become a better me.

I was on a road to living a healthier and happier life when I got the worst news that no one wants to hear – I found out that my mom had cancer in 2014. I was devastated and confused. How could this happen to a woman who never smoked or drank, and lived a healthy life? I decided to get on the plane and fly back home to be with my mom. I wanted to understand and learn everything about her lymphatic cancer.

After everything my mother had endured, from being married to an abusive husband and not enjoying everything in life, I couldn't stop wondering why this was happening to her. I didn't want to believe it when the doctor told me that my mom would die soon. I wanted to do anything I could to prolong her life. I changed her diet, cut sugar, and everything that was GMO modified.

This was a difficult time in my life. I was flying between Canada and Romania every six months to be with my mother as she went through her cancer treatments, and it took a toll on me. I needed to find a way to take care of myself and to find my healing. I was introduced to Reiki and it was so helpful. I decided to go to college for holistic training and became a Reiki master. I learned so much about how to control my breathing and how it can help heal the pain. I also learned about balancing chakras, the power of positive thinking, and how to change the way I see and react to life.

Despite my effort to try to get my mom to eat and live

healthier, she went back to her old lifestyle of poor eating habits. It was not long after this that I received the news that she died. After eight years, three surgeries, and radiation treatments, my mother had lost her battle with cancer in August 2020. I felt like my heart had been pulled out of my body. It has been the hardest thing for me to go through.

Imagine losing your mother during a worldwide pandemic and not being able to fly out to see her. Yes, my mom was there with some family members, but she's my mother and daughters always look up to their mothers. I wanted to be there to take away the pain she was going through. I felt hopeless and so sad without being able to be there for her final hour. I continued to pray for her as I always did. I didn't want her to die but, in my heart, I didn't want her to feel the pain and suffering anymore.

My mother's death has been the hardest part of my life. I felt like everything in my life stopped when she died. I couldn't eat. I had lost my best friend.

My mom meant everything to me. Not being able to fly home to be with her was so difficult. I was heartbroken because my final moment with my mom was with her on the phone. My best friend from Romania stayed with my mom until the last second of her life. She called me to tell me that my mom was about to pass away. I never felt so lost and don't think I will ever forget that moment. I was working that day and I don't know how I drove home. My friends came over one by one to stay with me and help comfort me. It meant so much to me to have my friends there for me during the hardest time of my life.

Unless you have gone through it, nobody knows what it is like to see and feel the pain of cancer on your loved one. In front of them, you show them that you are strong, but inside you feel hopeless and wish you had a cure to give them. As I mentioned, my mother never smoked or drank and she suffered so much in her final days. This was a dark time for me here in Canada, feeling hopeless because I was not able to fly to be by her side.

The airlines were blocked off, we were confined to our homes, and our government restricted travel to and from other countries. We were limited to leaving our homes only for essential products and services. Never would I have thought this would occur here in Canada or during my lifetime. I felt like I was back in Romania with these restrictions. I was stuck alone, crying about my mother being gone and feeling empty in a world of chaos, not knowing when this pandemic would end. Through all of this, I thank God my mother didn't have to suffer anymore. Today, I feel her presence all the time and see lovely birds that visit me on my Toronto condo balcony. I know she is so proud of me, loves me dearly, and looks out for me always!

Life can be complicated sometimes and we just have to figure out how to deal with it. I always strive to do what I love so that if I die tomorrow, I won't have regrets because I tried to enjoy every moment. I always like to buy the best food and beautiful clothes, and to travel to the places I've always dreamed of. I believe you should try to make peace with your past so that you can enjoy your future. Most of all, you should be kind to yourself and others.

I believe we have one shot and we should enjoy and love life. Our life is short and we have to do our best to live it fully. After the death of my mother, I focused on taking care of myself, eating healthy, and being grateful for everything and everyone. I didn't want to take anything for granted. I wanted to take the pain of losing my mother and turn it into something powerful for my future. A friend of mine once told me about different diets she's tried to get slimmer and how she came across a ketogenic diet. She suggested that I try it and I did. It has been two years and I still keep up my ketogenic lifestyle. I think it's the best thing I learned from my friend. I also assist others who are struggling to implement this change in their lives since I know the benefits as it helped me kick start my health journey!

Three years ago, I met Suzy Tamasy and I connected with more people who are trying as much as I am to be good and kind. Suzy works with helping women's shelters and empowering women to understand it's okay to start over again no matter where you are coming from or how difficult life has been. I don't like to tell people that I came from an abusive family, but I'm happy that I became strong enough to make a difference in my life. I feel privileged to be part of Suzy's empowering women program and I have to say that I'm so grateful to be doing something to help in making a difference. In my mom's memory, I will continue to be part of this amazing program. Thank you so much to Suzy for making this possible!

Suzy is a TV host for a show called *Empowered in Heels*, which she also has a magazine of that title, and which gave the name to this book. It is a show in which she interviews guests who empower others. When she approached me to be on her show, I asked if she would help me with what to say and she confirmed that there would be a set of questions.

After I did the interview, she said I was so incredible on her show! I ended up talking a bit about my experience as an older model and how important I think it is that we have more diverse models in the industry. One thing I have admired is Suzy's fashion line, *SuzyQJewels*, and that there is always a diverse range of models represented. Suzy believes there should be all shapes and ages of models. I truly felt empowered on her show since I was able to assist other models with their walk, style and encourage them that they can do it! I reflect on when I started modelling and wish I have had this type of support, so I now give that support to others.

I think of myself as a true fashionista! I love to dress up and style myself, which usually gets me tons of compliments. I relate to fashion as a way to be confident, look classy and stylish; a talent I've had since my younger years. I truly have a love affair with shoes and clothing and enjoy looking well put together. On Suzy's show, I felt empowered and in my element of doing what I love.

I have also had the opportunity to be one of the judges on *Empowered Models by SuzyQJewels*. I loved the chance to be a judge of fashion and style for the models. I was able to go behind the scenes to see their styling skills from when they received their attire and put accessories together. I got to observe their skills, teamwork, and confidence levels, as well as capture them empowering themselves with their makeup and hair, and with the photographers.

Working alongside a wide range of talent is truly rewarding for me. I get to do this with acting as well, but when the pandemic started this was another thing that I had to stop doing for a while. I missed it so much! Once we were finally told that we could proceed again, we had to do several Covid testing on set, isolate and do social distancing.

We only had the opportunity to work with our film bubble. Everyone thinks acting is easy but there are days I don't sleep or I am on set working in the cold, rain, or heat. It tends to be long hours and sometimes it's cumbersome when we have to do retakes or extend sets. You have to have a lot of patience and know-how to deal with so many different traits of characters.

Acting has its ups and downs, from having kind and good people on set to sometimes crossing paths with well-known actors whom you cannot speak with or the drama they put in place behind the scenes. When you go into acting, a waiver must be signed that says you cannot disclose who you meet and what you saw.

I believe we should make the best of any situation and not sweat over small things. Everyone has problems but it's all about how we respond to them. I believe in being happy and trying to be kind to everyone, including yourself. It's the most important thing you can do.

I have had great experiences in acting, modelling, and being a fashionista. My mother used to tell me to follow my dreams and I know she still checks up on me. I miss her and will love her forever! I know she is smiling from above, seeing my life blossom like a beautiful rose.

Dedication

I dedicate this story to my loving mother, Lona Cojocaru, who showed me to be strong, follow my dreams and never give up. This is in honour of her.

Looking out to the world Photography by Jolvi

Photography by Jolvi

Photographer Stan Trac

"*Energy* is the essence of life. Every day you decide how you're going to use it by knowing what you want and what it takes to reach the goal, and by maintaining focus."

- Oprah Winfrey

Long Road Home

Written by Jennifer Traynor, as told by Cheryl Bailey

Do you know how sometimes people can describe something as a blessing in disguise? Well, that's exactly how I feel about a back injury I sustained a few years ago. I didn't know it at the time, but this would be a moment that would completely change the course of my life's path, and in turn, would become a life experience that I am now truly grateful for. Though, to share how my back injury was a blessing in disguise, I need to go back a bit further in my life to give you a bit of insight on how I reached this point in my journey.

I've always thought of myself as a perceptive person. I tend to be able to read people easily and get a sense of the essence of who they are. Growing up, my mother was a foster parent and she would always welcome the children into our home with open arms. She would treat them with compassion and kindness. She would show them that they were valued, and they knew they were in a safe and loving home. This experience helped me understand how all people are worthy of love and respect, and from then on, this was the lens through which I would view the world and the people I met.

Perhaps this aspect of my personality is what drew me to be a creative person.

I've always been attracted to the arts, and growing up I often enjoyed painting and photography, so much so that I eventually went into studying fine arts. I love being creative! It's the one way that I feel I can best express myself and my interpretation of the world around me. Art can tell a story or portray emotions in a way that transcends language, allowing anyone to understand the meaning behind it. In its beautiful way, art connects humankind, and this is why I feel so blessed to have tapped into this part of who I am.

Despite my love of being artistic and creative, continuing with my fine arts studies was not meant to be. After losing my mom as a young teen and taking on the role of helping to raise my younger brother, I had to shift gears when it came to planning my future. This loss forced me to grow up faster than any teenager is intended to. I had suddenly gone from being a kid to filling the shoes of a responsible adult and mother figure, and I started to view my life a bit differently. I chose to put my passion for the arts aside and take a more practical approach to my future by going on to become a social worker. Due to my experience of the foster care system that I had with my mom when she was a foster parent, as well as my natural way of connecting with people, I found this to be a good choice and a step in the right direction.

I began my career in social work, but also continued to dabble in photography, and even ended up doing apprenticeships with three different Toronto photographers for a while. One of the main things that I learned from these photographers was how to find my unique style and how I would capture my subjects through the lens. While I learned a lot as an apprentice, I also took the initiative to learn the ins and outs of photography on my own. The more I learned, the more I wanted to continue doing photography in some capacity, so I decided to work as a photographer part-time while still working full-time as a social worker.

My years as a counsellor with social services gave me many opportunities to work with various organizations, and even volunteer with grassroots organizations and with the homeless. This is something I continue to do today and have gotten my children involved in volunteering with me. Giving back to the community has always been important to me. It is something I know that was instilled in me by my mother and an important lesson that I now pass along to my family.

My photography has played a large role in my volunteer work, as I have often given my time to photograph events. This has been a beautiful way to combine my two passions: helping others and being behind the camera. For over 20 years, I was able to fulfill these two passions through my full-time job as a social worker and being a photographer part-time. The more I volunteered my time to photograph events, the more people would find out about what I did, and in turn, I saw my part-time photography business grow. Being able to give back to the community, to be of service to others, all while still being able to express my artistic and creative side, was extremely satisfying. Life was good!

As a social worker, I had many opportunities to connect with helping others, but I was especially drawn to helping troubled youth. Perhaps this stemmed from watching my mother in her role as a foster parent, or perhaps it was from the fact that I lost part of my youth when I lost my mom at such a young age. Either way, I felt a great deal of accomplishment when I was able to work with young people. I have a way of seeing their potential, while others may look past it. Our youth need to feel seen and heard; they need to know they are worthy and that they matter. As a social worker, I have witnessed troubled youth being dismissed and faded into the background. If I can be that one person who will believe in them and give them the lift that they need, then I will be that person.

One such opportunity presented itself back in 2011. I was assigned to work with some teens, many of them young women or teen moms, at an alternative school, and the experience had a deep impact on me. Seeing that these troubled youth were treated with so much respect and as if they mattered was incredibly inspirational. There was a genuine interest in seeing these youth succeed and I was so impressed with the empowerment that these young women received.

As I continued my social work there, I ended up getting permission to photograph these teens. Their stories moved me and I wanted to capture them, showcase them, and celebrate them. This was how I came up with the idea to put it all in a book. With the consent of the alternative school and these teen girls, I created a photo book to spotlight their incredible stories. Along with the photographs I took, I asked these young ladies to write poems about self-confidence and what it means to be happy to showcase alongside their pictures. I did this all voluntarily and decided all the proceeds from the sale of the book would go back to helping these phenomenal young women. I titled the book *Roots* because it highlighted where they came from and how they were sprouting into the world. Not only did working on the *Roots* book project inspire me as a woman, but it also motivated me as a photographer. Right then and there I knew that my photos would be my unique way of storytelling, and my photography mission statement was born: It is my job to capture your story through a lens.

From there, I began capturing wonderful stories through my photography with a variety of clients. I did mainly lifestyle photoshoots, such as maternity, mom and baby, and weddings. With this being my side hustle, I had the flexibility to pick and choose the jobs I wanted to work on and tailor them to my full-time social work schedule. I was feeling extremely fulfilled in my life with the ability to have the combination of doing two things that I was so passionate about – helping others through social work and expressing my creative side through the camera. Until one day in 2014, everything changed.

My life came to a halt when I sustained a serious back injury and found out I would require surgery. I had to take a long leave of absence from work while I recovered. It was a challenging time. The uncertainty of whether I could go back to doing the work I loved left me feeling unsettled, and once I found out the company that I had worked for wasn't going to be able to make the accommodations needed for me to return to my social services job, I was left feeling lost and unsure of what my next step would be. My first main goal was to recover from my injury and surgery, which took a lot of determination.

This ended up being a time of deep reflection as I found myself going through a bit of an identity crisis. For so long, I had thought that social work was my purpose in life, and not being able to return to it had me questioning everything I knew. I needed to find a way to turn this negative situation into a positive one, and so I began contemplating the idea of becoming a full-time photographer. Being behind the camera has been a part of my life for so long, so why not take this opportunity to turn something that I'm passionate about into my career? Perhaps this was where life was leading me all along, and photography was my true purpose. I decided to go for it! While it was a scary decision to make, I felt it was time to make the change. Taking that leap of faith was probably the best thing I could have done.

When I was working as a photographer part-time, I was selective about the jobs that I took, but now working at it full-time means that I can be more open about the clients I work with and the jobs that I do. I love the more natural side of lifestyle photography, like taking candid shots or capturing intimate moments and emotions. I enjoy making my photoshoots fun and playful for the people I work with. I want my clients to feel relaxed and at ease. Once they do, the magic happens and that's when I get to create some wonderful portraits. I'm lucky enough to witness it and feel blessed to capture these memories people will cherish for years to come.

In the past, I had always put barriers up and played it safe. I feel ready now to stop saying "No" to myself and see where it takes me. With every YES that I put out into the universe; more opportunities came my way. The perfect example is when the chance to get into fashion photography came to me in late 2019. I had never shot fashion before and was excited to challenge myself in this way. I have done many fashion photoshoots since then and have gained a newfound respect for the industry and everything that goes on behind the scenes.

I love working with professional models, makeup artists, designers, and clothes. It's a collaboration and there is so much energy! There are demands, pressure, expectations, and deadlines, but the excitement and creativity of it all are amazing! It keeps me on my toes and I love it!

It's funny how one moment in life can change everything. If I hadn't sustained my back injury, I wouldn't have made a full-time career as a photographer, and in turn, these exciting opportunities might not have come my way. I possibly would not have challenged myself to explore this area of my life further and may have missed out on discovering the full potential of what I can do. When we are faced with difficult moments in life, we often can't see the possibility of the good they can bring. Yet, if we allow ourselves to be open-minded, we could be surprised by the outcome.

I believe in being true to yourself, standing up for yourself, and the power of being heard. I always encourage others to be strong and fierce in what they do. I believe in living a life of serving others, treating everyone I meet with respect and kindness, and I pride myself on teaching my children to do the same.

I have learned so much from this life so far, and how the good and bad times have lessons to teach us. My journey has taught me how resilient I am, and what I'm capable of achieving. When I look back on the path that is now behind me, I'm grateful for everything that came along the way, bumps and all. These experiences helped shape the woman I am today. When I look ahead on the path yet to come, I'm filled with hope and have faith in where it will lead me. I am blessed to be on this journey surrounded by so many amazing people who love and support me. They are the ones who inspire and motivate me, and they are also those who make taking a leap of faith all worthwhile.

Dedication

I would like to dedicate this story, my story, to all the significant people who have helped shape my journey thus far.

To my mother for setting the example that I have and always will follow – seek out and find the good in people, to always be kind because everyone has a story.

To my husband, children, family members, and friends who continue to inspire me, encourage me, support me and love me throughout all of life's ups and downs.

To the photographers who've guided and mentored me.

To those in my life who never gave up on me, and instead, kept pushing me to reach for the stars.

To the clients whom I've learned from, helped, and who, in turn, helped me.

To the people, the families, who have entrusted me to capture their most precious moments.

To myself for not giving up and saying "YES!" to new opportunities and "NO" to the fear that tries to stop me.

I'd like to end off with a quote from one of my favourite songs, *Kind & Generous* by Natalie Merchant – to all the people I've mentioned above, this is for you:

"Oh, I want to thank you for so many gifts you gave;

The love, the tenderness, I want to thank you.

I want to thank you for your generosity, the love

And the honesty that you gave me.

I want to thank you show, my gratitude

My love, and my respect for you, I want to thank you.

Oh, I want to thank you, thank you, thank you, thank you;

I want to thank you, thank you, thank you, thank you."

Cheryl Bailey

Our Son & Father Photo for Father's Day done by Me
published in Biz & Fashion Magazine

Photo of my Gals

Savanah Sargent

Daughter/Model EM.T Photo done by me at Divas In Durham

Daughter/Model EM.T Photo done by me at Divas In Durham

Following My Dreams and Turning Them into Reality

By Demi Theo

Born in Greece, I immigrated to Canada and settled in Toronto with my family when I was nine years old. Although placed in an English-speaking school, I did not speak the English language and was placed in ESL classes in school. It was here that I encountered problems with my classmates, who bullied and teased me for not speaking English fluently.

As I write this, I remember being bullied a lot during my school years and I'm reminded of one particular incident when a classmate stuck chewing gum in my ponytail. My mother had to cut out a chunk of the hair, as there was no other way to remove the gum. Another time, during recess, a student started kicking me for no reason, except to show off in front of his friends. Of course, my parents always protected me and made

69

sure the teachers and principal of the school were made aware of this and did something about these occurrences.

Although my parents were strict, making sure I did my homework first after school, they were always very fair, which I appreciate to this day. Education was very important to my parents, who had immigrated from Greece for better opportunities, but once my homework was done, I could then watch my favourite TV shows, or play.

Growing up, I found television to be both entertaining and educational and I loved watching children's entertainment and educational shows, not just to learn English, but to make all the crafts that were demonstrated on these shows. I was also a very independent, fit, and active child. I started walking to school by myself from an early age and participating in various sporting activities like volleyball, swimming, and tennis. My favourite sport was bowling, having been taught by my dad it became a favourite activity on weekends, after church service.

My dad loved driving, and he took the family out every weekend. Niagara Falls was a family favorite. I have fond memories of the many days spent there exploring parks, museums, rides, and even going further sometimes to swim at Crystal Beach. I always enjoyed visiting the annual summer exhibition in downtown Toronto with my family each summer and have fond memories from the many times when my parents' friends and their children joined together into a large group of 20 or more people to spend precious quality time together at the events and occasions held there.

As an 'A-grade' student, I won numerous awards at school. I developed the hobby of writing short stories to help me learn the English language, which also helped me maintain my good grades, and my teachers often commented on my imagination and creativity. One particular summer, I wrote a mini science-fiction novel titled *The Head Without a Body,* which was about a scientist who kept an actual head of a person alive through the wonders of science. My story was inspired by a horror movie I'd seen while watching late-night movies with my mom on the weekends.

Growing up, I had many dreams about what career I would follow, and while my interests varied widely, including teaching, art, fashion, and modelling, I also had dreams of being a flight attendant or a police officer as I love to challenge myself. My parents instilled a strong work ethic in me, and I was raised to not be afraid of hard work, as well as to help others, which often got me involved in fundraising for worthy causes from a young age. During my high school years, I was eager to get a job and started my first job as a cashier at a fast-food restaurant when I turned 16.

High school was a far less traumatic experience for me and I have good memories of getting together with friends at lunchtime for fun or to do homework. I worked in the evenings during my free time to save enough money to pay for my future education. Upon completing grade 13, with honours, I was accepted into the interior design program at a well-known university in downtown Toronto.

Before attending university, I completed two architectural drafting courses at two different colleges during my summer breaks. I found the interior design course to be challenging and competitive, and often found myself going without sleep for up to 48 hours straight to complete projects, but I did not mind as my passion for design was my driving force. Sometimes, my department collaborated with the fashion department or the hospitality and tourism department which made the experience all the more fun.

Upon completing the four-year program, I graduated with honours with a Bachelors' degree in Applied Arts and was pleased when I was invited back to the school the following

71

year to present a lecture to the then fourth-year students who were writing a thesis.

I remember how shy I was when one of the requirements was to do public speaking during my thesis in my fourth year. I had to present my thesis to an audience of unknown people from the public, but despite the nerves and my voice cracking, I managed to do very well on the project. By the time I lectured the fourth-year class, I had gained more confidence in public speaking due to completing an English Literature mini-course at a west end university that required a lot of speed reading and presentations, which proved to be good practice for me.

My thesis was based on a Greek-inspired community centre of my own design, complete with a nursing home, daycare centre, gym, an amphitheatre, and restaurant. The setting of this community centre was at the beautiful bluffs on Lake Ontario as it is reminiscent of Greece. As part of my thesis, I also researched and composed a book appropriately entitled *Mount Olympus Socio-Cultural Centre*, which was registered under copyright law as an "unpublished literary and artistic work," a bound hard copy of which still sits in the university library.

Once I completed my degree, I obtained my first design job at a construction company in midtown Toronto, working on the drafting of projects and assisting with the design of kiosks and stores in Edmonton, Alberta, where I later travelled to. I also helped design these stores at a mall in Hamilton. Following this, I went on to work for an architectural firm where one of my jobs was to assist with the interior design of a medical professional building in downtown Toronto. During this time, and while I was working two jobs, the architectural firm and a part-time evening job as a supermarket cashier, I met my future husband. In the first years of our marriage, we travelled across the world extensively, only settling down once our two daughters came along, at which point the travelling stopped and the family remained local until the girls were old enough.

I stopped working since I wanted to raise our daughters myself without the need for daycare and babysitters. I believed in giving them precious time with their parents and helping them grow up in a secure environment while learning two languages – first the mother tongue, Greek, then English, which I knew would come easily once they started school. I did this to ensure that my daughters knew their Greek heritage, as well as to enable them to communicate with their grandparents, which I did by driving them to Greek school to study the language and culture each Saturday.

Unfortunately, my marriage ended in divorce when our daughters were aged 6 and 12. Now left totally on my own, with two young children to care for, I accepted the first job I was offered at a small telemarketing company offering sales work. On my first evening on the job, and knowing nothing about telemarketing, I did not get any sales, but I vowed to myself that I would not fail, and would do my utmost to succeed. By the second night, I had achieved my first sale and was thrilled when my colleagues and the management team started applauding loudly to show their support. I found this truly inspiring. From then on, I never left the office without getting a sale, and my perseverance paid off.

To ensure that I was financially secure, I held down a part-time day job as well in a retail chain store while the children were at school. I would pick up my kids, bring them home and help with homework before making my way to my evening job. Luckily, when my eldest daughter was of an age to assist me with babysitting duties for my youngest daughter, I knew I had her support and this enabled me to maintain our standard of living as a single parent holding down two jobs.

In 2012, I was fortunate enough to meet the owner of a company dealing with health and wellness products. They took an immediate liking to me and asked me to model for some corporate brochures due to my exotic appearance, which eventually lead to me being the face of the brand, as well as a Brand Ambassador. This included me being the photographic model for their catalogue and advertising campaign, as well as a PR sales representative demonstrating products, such as whole-body vibration machines, infra-red saunas, and handheld massagers.

This eventually led to more modelling opportunities. In 2016, I got to fulfill my lifelong dream of being a fashion model when I was invited to be a runway model for a popular local fashion show. The event is organized by a leading member of the Toronto Greek community who has been the organizer for this show for more than two decades. Growing up, my parents frowned upon modelling as a career option and I was discouraged from participating in it.

As an adult, I found it quite liberating to fulfill this lifelong dream and went on to repeat it when I returned in 2018 to the runway of that same fashion show, which had a live audience of over 800 people and was televised across Canada and Greece.

In 2018, the founder of a new fashion show in Toronto geared just for kids asked me to join her as a co-organizer for the inaugural event to be held in December of that year. This would be the very first kind of kids' fashion show event to be held in Toronto. Its founder was already familiar with my strength and skills in sales and marketing, and she quickly involved me in recruiting fashion designers, sponsors, photographers, make-up artists, vendors, and VIP invitations for the launch of the first show.

It turned out to be one of the most successful fashion events of 2018, attracting over 1,000 attendees at a venue in downtown Toronto.

I managed to entice several internationally and locally renowned fashion and accessory designers to participate at this event, which included an international eco-friendly fashion designer amongst other big local and out-of-town designers. This important bi-annual event prides itself in promoting diversity in the fashion and modelling sector and strives to inspire and empower young models and fashionistas of the future. I am proud to continue to co-organize this event!

In the last 10 years, my career seems to have gained momentum as I start to fulfill many of my childhood dreams in the field for which I have so much passion.

I went as far as taking a short fashion design course alongside my older daughter. Not only did I have loads of fun, but I got to design a versatile outfit – one that could be worn eight different ways. I also got to model it at the final class exhibit.

In early 2019, I was invited to participate as a model for another big fashion show in Toronto. That same year, one of the organizers of a big dance studio hired me to help promote a huge event in the city. This event consisted of bringing the best dance-duos in Latin-American and Ballroom dance from countries across Europe under one roof in Markham, Ontario. I found myself talking on live radio alongside the event organizer promoting the event, attending its fundraiser dance, and being present at the press conference.

Soon, my life in the fashion world expanded from the runway to the magazine pages. The editor of *Spencer Magazine* asked me to write an article for his digital publication. With his encouragement, I wrote my first magazine article about a fashion event that I also modelled in.

One article turned into two, and then three, until finally, in 2020, I was hired as a columnist for *Biz & Fashion Magazine*, a stylish glossy magazine with over 10,000 subscribers worldwide that benefits local women's shelters and small businesses. For the column, I create fashion-related crafts and model them. The column is titled *DIY by De Tee*, making use of my social media pseudonym which represents my initials; hence some people sometimes call me De, short for Demi.

When the Covid-19 pandemic hit, and we went into lockdowns, I decided to focus on my craft column and quickly came to realize that with the libraries, book stores, and schools closed, children could not attend reading groups and story time circles read by the dedicated librarians. I used to love reading as a young girl as it took my imagination to far-away places and I dreamed of writing my own book someday, so with that in mind, I started my own YouTube channel called *Demi's Story and Craft Time*. For the inaugural story time video, I chose the book *Goldilocks and The Three Bears* and used my handmade characters and crafts, as well as narrating, as a test run. As the editor and producer for my YouTube channel, my life-long friend Cesar Casillas Flores helped me debut my first story in December 2020, which achieved over 1500 views in a very short time. The success of this first video encouraged me to continue doing craft-related stories and I remembered a children's story I'd written some years ago. After much hunting, I found the original, and that was how the story of *The Magical Chickadee* was born. This story has a special meaning for me as I wrote it when my daughter was young, and based the main character, Stacy, on my daughter. The characters of Stacy's grandparents are based on my parents.

Once I had completed the story and crafted the various characters and scenes, I then stylized the sets and photographed them. Next, I asked my friend Tracey McLean-Low, who is a writer, to proofread and edit it for self-publishing. She suggested that I write a series of at least five stories for professional publication, and we teamed up to create *The Magical Chickadee & Friends*. By March of 2021, I had done a collection of stories and crafts, starting with *The Valentine Bears*, which inspired me to create a miniature dollhouse. This was quickly followed by its sequel, *The Valentine Bears Vacation*, where the Valentines went on a much-deserved vacation. Next came *The Ferpinderps*, which is based on an idea from my youngest daughter. Finally came the story of *Mrs. Fuzzy Jazzy and The Case of The Missing Designer Bag*, which is a fashion-based story.

After two months of editing and publication design work, and with the help of many sponsors, a limited sample edition of *The Magical Chickadee & Friends (Stories & Crafts by Demi Theo)* was published in time for Easter weekend of 2021. Soon after, the premiere of the YouTube video for *The Magical Chickadee* was produced. It was during this time that Suzy Tamasy invited me to be a guest on her TV show *Empowered in Heels*, a well-produced talk show focusing on the empowerment of women. Suzy interviewed me about the evolution of my children's book *The Magical Chickadee*, as well as my crafting, my involvement with the children's fashion show, and being the DIY columnist for *Biz & Fashion Magazine*. I also demonstrated how to make a craft live on the show.

Looking back over the last few years of my career is proving to be a dream come true, and I am proud of the woman that my inner child has become. I appreciate the opportunities I have been given that are enabling me to achieve the many things my childhood dreams inspired me to do. I have loved fashion from an early age and I loved to play dress-up. Living in Europe during my formative years, I was exposed to the styles and fashion from the Paris and London fashion weeks, so later on, when I had saved enough of my allowance money, I splurged on a celebrity doll, which was popular at the time. This purchase would later turn out to be the first of a large doll

collection that now includes a range of limited-edition fashion dolls and porcelain dolls. My love of crafting came from my great aunt who custom-made most of my outfits, which were stitched with great skill, and who had a creative talent for dressmaking and handmade crafts.

Over the years I have studied all things related to the art and fashion world, which also gave me an appreciation for history and architecture, as well as great artists in history. While I get my inspiration from the greats, I get my best ideas from situations and observations of daily life, and with a little imagination and transformation, they begin to take shape.

All the materials I use for my DIY crafts are made from used and recycled articles or scrap pieces of materials. Anything I find interesting I will save it in my craft bag for something to make later. I can make something beautiful from what other people would see as garbage, but I see the potential and importance of everything.

I firmly believe that effort, time, patience, and perseverance are the keys to achieving your dreams. I also believe in the importance of having a good work/life balance and making sure to spend quality time with family and friends, as well as enjoy the finer things in life. I take great pride in having created a lifestyle career, but it took a lot of effort and endurance for me to start to accomplish my dreams. I have merely scratched the surface in the last 10 years of what I feel I still have left to achieve.

I try to enjoy life to the fullest and hope to be as inspirational to the next generation as previous generations have been for me. While I have turned many of my hobbies into a career, I continue to enjoy art, crafts, gardening, cooking, modelling, show production, people, and event management, alongside enjoying an active family and social life. My positive attitude is what enables me to now be able to enjoy a fulfilling lifestyle, even during the most trying of times, from divorce to pandemics.

Thinking positively can help turn negative experiences into positive outcomes. I like to see the best in everything and will keep striving to pursue my lifelong dreams. With so many exciting and challenging experiences over the last decade, I hope to keep turning my dreams into reality. As I was quoted in the April 2021 edition of *Isabella Magazine*, "you have to follow your dreams, never give up no matter what age you are," and I will keep doing exactly that.

Dedication

I dedicate this to all the beautiful people in my life that helped me develop into the person I am today, the most important of all being my parents. Family means everything to me! To the first and primary woman in my life, my mother, who always cared for me, gave me her unconditional love, and who always took the time and patience to listen to me and give me her best advice whenever I needed it, and still does to this day! To my father, who was a great family man, and who always took care of me and my younger brother and our mom of course! He was very strict at times when I was growing up and I didn't understand this, but in my later years, I grew to realize that he knew exactly what he was doing. He raised me well, taught me a lot of values, and today I am grateful for the person that I am because of both my parents.

To my only sibling, my younger brother – I am proud to have you in my life! When I was little, one of my dreams was to become a teacher, but you ended up being the teacher. I am proud that you have followed your dream and have been working as a successful teacher who is loved by all. As you were growing up, you always looked up to me and you have learned a lot from me. Although you are much younger than me, you always have supported me, and still do in a lot of ways, which I truly appreciate.

To my gorgeous, smart, wise, and thoughtful sister-in-law, the pharmacist in our family – I'm so proud to have you in our family!

To my outgoing, well-mannered nephews – I am proud of both of you and your achievements.

Of course, last but not least, to my two beautiful, wonderful daughters who have also fulfilled my life and made it worth living with a purpose. My wish for you is that you both follow your dreams and turn them into reality, and do not let any obstacles stop you. I hope for you to be independent, as it is the best thing that you can do for yourself. Love yourself first, so that you can enable yourself to help others. Always do good and think positive, because positivity in thought brings positivity in life, and never be afraid to try new things and enjoy your lives!

Always believe in yourself and exercise your inner strength. Do not be afraid to push the limits of your abilities. You will eventually find out that, yes, you can rely on yourself, because, after all, it is true what they say: "Behind every successful man there is a good woman...but behind every successful woman there is herself!"

I also dedicate this to all my wonderful friends, of whom there have been many, and you know who you are! Throughout my life, I have been blessed with really good friends that have kept me well grounded. They always inspired me in life, kept me smiling, and were continuously encouraging, good listeners, good company, and fun people to be with. I feel it is important to have a good set of friends. Once, when I was about 12 years old, I had embroidered a wall hanging. It was cross-stitched. On it was the words "Make new friends but keep the old. The new are silver, the old ones are gold."

I still have that hanging on my wall. I hope my story inspires people of all ages. Enjoy reading! Wishing you all peace, love, good health, and happiness! ~ *Demi Theo*

Photocredit Jaime Leigh Bigham

De
mi MC

Pictured Demi Theo, author, model and cover of Biz & Fashion
Magazine

Demi at age 18

Stories and Crafts
By Demi Theo

We would like to express our sincerest gratitude for celebrating our Welcome Spring and "The Magical Chickadee - Stories and Crafts" by: Demi Theo

As a young girl, I always enjoyed reading, as it took my imagination into far away places. I always dreamed of writing my very own book some day.

When the pandemic struck in early 2020, everything suddenly closed - including public libraries.

My idea to form my own youtube channel - "Demis Story and Craft Time"evolved when I narrated the first story, "Goldilocks and The Three Bears" using my hand made characters and crafts. I was very happy with it but then I thought, "Why not write my own stories?"

I remembered I wrote a childrens story some years ago - I searched for it and found it. I polished it up; and low and behold "The Magical Chickadee" was born!

My editor , Tracey McLean- Low, encouraged me to write a series of at least five stories and soon I came up with this collection , and the rest is history.

There were some major people that helped inspire me to develop my writing further - Joseph Edward Schur who encouraged me to write my very first magazine article and published the few I wrote in SPENCER MAGAZINE, and Rose Marie Bresolin who edited them. Ola Dominuco, has also published my articles in her magazine "Isabella."

And last but not least, Suzy Tamasy who made me a columnist for "DIY by De Tre" Written by Demi Theo each month in BIZ & FASHION MAGAZINE, and also published some articles in the same publication. The editor of the latter magazine , Suzy Tamasy, gave me her blessing; she wished me to "reach for the stars" ! Very valuable advice to me coming from the editor of a magazine that has reached over 10k audience worldwide! Thank you, Suzy! That is exactly what I will aim to do! My writing journey has just begun!

Author & Model Demi Theo
Photocredit Mo Zee

THE MAGICAL CHICKADEE & FRIENDS

STORIES & CRAFTS BY DEMI THEO
© 2021

April 2021, featuring The Magical Chickadee and Friends Stories and crafts by Demi Theo. Photo credit: Mo Zee of Mo Zee Photo Services Attire: Suzyqjewels

Demi in Suzyqjewels attire
Photo credit: Aesha Malik of Your Product Your Shot Studios

SUZYQJEWELS

Do something good for you and others we support Women Shelters.

SUZY TAMASY
FOUNDER & CEO

416 262-0816
suzyqjewels@gmail.com

Learning to Love Myself

By Jennifer Traynor

Have you ever felt so lost that you didn't even know who you were anymore? This was my experience. I had many titles to describe me – daughter, sister, wife, mother, friend, employee – but when it came right down to it, I couldn't find the right words to describe me, the *real* me. The biggest problem was that for so many years I had let other people define who I was. I had navigated my way through life, going through the different stages, and along the way had completely lost sight of my own identity. I simply went through the motions of my day, playing each role how I thought I should. I used the words of how others described me as the definition of who 'Jennifer' was.

Now and then, I would recognize this problem but would never really deal with it head-on. I would push it aside because I had more important things to worry about. I had the responsibilities of being a wife and mother, going to work, paying the bills, and taking care of our home. I had people counting on me, and in my mind, they came first. I could focus on myself later. But here's the thing. When later came and I did take some time to think about myself, and what I wanted, I was met with so many different emotions. Mainly, I was left with the bad ones. I didn't like who I was, and when I would allow myself to think deeply about this, it meant acknowledging the fact that I couldn't think of a time when I truly loved myself.

Years of self-deprecation led to living life feeling full of anger, disappointment, and frustration. I was able to "fake it until you make it" for a very long time. On the outside, I appeared to be this calm, happy woman, when on the inside I was a complete mess. I kept pushing forward in life, trying desperately to hold it together and just accepting that this was how my life would be. I mean, it had been this way for such a long time so why would it change now? But I couldn't hold it together any longer. The strands of who I was began to unravel and I couldn't tie them back up. The broken pieces of me were about to come crashing down. I didn't know it then, but my life was about to change in a big way.

It all started one March morning. I had just gotten out of the shower and as I looked in the mirror, I realized I didn't recognize the woman staring back at me. Who was this shell of a woman in the reflection? There were dark circles around my eyes and an empty expression that displayed no emotion, and yet at the same time, I felt so much. It was like at that moment the heaviness of what I was feeling was too much to hold in anymore, to the point that I just had to let it all out.

I slowly crumpled to the floor, my chest heaving from the sobs. I wanted to pound my fists and wail at the top of my lungs, but with my children and husband downstairs I opted to release this pain quietly. At that moment, all of the anguish, frustration, sadness, disappointment, and anger came pouring out of me. I cried for what seemed like hours. Maybe it was hours, who knows. It was long enough that my husband came upstairs to check on me because I had been in there for so long. He walked in to find me on the bathroom floor, my face puffy from sobbing. I looked at him with tear-stained cheeks and said, "I think I need help."

My husband knew that I'd been struggling. Heck, how could he not? Every day I woke up already irritable and I often took out my bad mood on him and the kids. It hurts me to know how my actions impacted them and the pain I likely caused.

I shudder with disappointment and regret every time I think about how I would yell at the kids and be so short-tempered with my husband. How could I have been such an ugly person to the most important people in my life? I am grateful every day for their forgiveness, compassion, love, and support. I wouldn't have gotten to the point I'm at today without them.

Though my husband knew I was having a tough time, this particular day was the first time I admitted to him that I had depression. He told me he suspected this was the case but that he was unsure how to approach the subject. As he held me in his arms, I told him I was going to seek help and he assured me that we would get through this together.

The next day I saw my family doctor. As I waited in the small examination room for her, I remember feeling completely numb. I felt nothing. I felt lost. I felt like I wanted to run away, but I knew I needed to be there. When she finally walked into the room it was like she instantly knew something was wrong.

Or perhaps I just looked *that* horrible. She immediately asked if I was okay. I opened my mouth, trying to find the words to say, but all that came out were more sobs. She quietly and patiently waited, handing me a tissue, and when I finally was able to catch my breath, I looked at her and said "I think I have depression. Please help me."

I left the doctor's office with a prescription for antidepressants and the urging from my doctor to find a therapist immediately. My doctor included instructions for my diet, sleep, and exercise to ensure that I was taking care of myself. She also instructed me to come back to see her in three months. She wanted to see for herself the progress I'd make and continue my care from there.

She made it clear that the medication would not be the only solution to dealing with my depression and expressed the importance of getting additional help along with taking care of my body and mind by staying healthy.

I started the antidepressants the same day and within a few weeks, I was in therapy. My first session with my therapist was intense. During that first conversation, we uncovered some deep pain that had been buried inside; pain that I couldn't ignore anymore and that I needed to finally face and let go of.

This pain was rooted in my childhood, from a time when I had been tormented and bullied. As a child I let the words of my bullies define me – stupid, ugly, worthless. I had allowed that to be my definition through my teens and adulthood. What I regret more is that I had permitted my worst critic to stick by me, day in and day out, as I navigated my life, providing a dark narrative along the way.

Why did I let this bully stick around? What was it going to take for her to finally go away? My therapist pointed out that this was not going to be an easy task and I knew she was right. This was going to require me to gather up a lot of courage and strength to fight for myself since my bully had been following me around for years, constantly telling me that I wasn't enough. I knew her well because that bully was me.

From there, my healing journey was like a roller coaster ride, full of dips, twists, and turns. The antidepressants helped to stabilize my moods and therapy helped me uncover the work I needed to do. My primary focus was learning to love who I am. After a lot of talking with my therapist and much reflection, my lack of self-esteem appeared to be the root of many of my problems. I had somehow made it to my mid-thirties having absolutely no faith in myself. I never believed that I could truly be happy and achieve great things. I was always putting myself down. This was an eye-opening discovery. For so many years, I kept focusing on what I didn't have rather than on what I did have. I spent a great deal of time complaining about how I was not getting anywhere in my career and how I always seemed to be wanting something more in my life, despite having a wonderful husband, beautiful kids, and a lovely home.

Yet, I kept dwelling on my career and I couldn't see the reason why I kept hitting dead ends. The thing is, how could I expect anyone to believe in me if I didn't believe in myself?

Years of low self-esteem and self-doubt had taken a toll on me, body, mind, and spirit. Going through therapy helped me see that I was my personal punching bag for a very long time. Through every failure in my life – failed friendships and romantic relationships, or my attempts at attaining my dream job – I blamed myself. I was convinced that all of these failures were the result of me not being good enough to deserve better. Even with a loving husband and my two children, I often wondered how I could be worthy of them. I remember asking my husband on more than one occasion why he loved me because I honestly believed I wasn't worth loving. I had many moments of believing my family was truly better off without me and had countless moments of weakness where I was so tempted to run away.

I can recall one time in particular driving home from work. I had a horrible day. Nothing, in particular, had happened to make it a bad day. It was just one of those low points along my journey with depression. It was raining, which made traffic move at a snail's pace. As I sat in my car, slowly inching toward home, my mind wandered, as it often does when I'm driving alone. Soon, tears were streaming down my face. I was so tired – tired of feeling sadness and disappointment. I was tired of dealing with the stress of being at a job I didn't like, and the soul-sucking task of job hunting. I was tired of the responsibilities of motherhood. I was tired of the heaviness I felt in my life. As I wiped away my tears, I sat there fantasizing about how my life might change if I just ran away, reinvented myself, and left this life behind me. As traffic picked up, I soon found myself driving past my exit off the highway. I just wanted to keep driving and see where the road took me. I had this brief moment of relief before this voice in my head shouted, "what the hell are you doing?" I kept driving a bit longer, in a daze, before the tears sprung to my eyes again. "This isn't the answer,"

I said out loud to myself. I knew running away wouldn't change anything and that my troubles wouldn't be left behind. The depression would follow me no matter where I went. This was a fact unless I did the work my doctor and therapist urged me to do to get better. More importantly, things wouldn't change until I stopped the self-loathing and started discovering the wonderful woman buried inside. I got off the highway, turned around, and drove straight home.

I made a promise to myself that from that point forward I needed to try very hard to think differently of myself and my life. I made goals with my therapist about how I was going to take control of making changes instead of waiting for them to happen. One of the first things I decided was that it was time for me to pursue what makes me happy. I would start making those shifts so that I could get on track with a career I love. Writing has always been a passion of mine, ever since I was a child.

When I went to college for print journalism my dream was to one day become the editor of a magazine. Yet, there I was almost 15 years into my career since graduating and I had managed to stray away from that path. It's not like I had diverted far but it was far enough that I felt I needed to start fresh.

The first step I took was starting a blog. I was so out of practice with my writing and wanted to get back into it regularly. I thought blogging, even if I had hardly any readers, was a good way to get back to writing, and potentially build up a portfolio as I looked for work as a writer. I started a mom blog in early 2016, building the website by myself, creating all of the content, as well as making connections with other publications and companies to try to get my work featured. For nearly two years, I tried getting a job writing, but with no luck. Despite feeling incredibly discouraged I kept trying and hoping that finally, I would find a perfectly suited writing job for me, until one day it happened. I got hired as a copywriter for a parenting publication in August 2017. I was beyond excited.

This was the job I had been waiting for! After a long journey of working hard and searching, I felt like I had finally found the perfect job that was meant for me.

I spent every day writing and editing, collaborating with my team, and coming up with creative ideas. I loved it! I started to see my moods getting better and my confidence growing. For the first time in a long time, I was beginning to feel like I was finding the real me. Although I was still struggling a bit with my depression, I felt as though I was getting a better handle on coping. However, just as quickly as things changed for the good, my life took another dip. Nine months after getting what I thought was my dream job, I was laid off. Right after getting the news over the phone from my boss, I found myself sobbing on the floor yet again. Losing my job hit me so hard that I felt like I was pushed right back to the bottom of the hole I had myself in just a few years before. There I was, back in this dark place and I had no idea how I was going to climb out.

The months following being laid off were rough. I experienced so many emotions. I was so confused. Why did this happen? Why would life send me this wonderful opportunity only to have it yanked away? I started questioning everything about the goals and decisions I had made just a couple of years ago with my therapist. Had I chosen the right path, or had I set myself up for disappointment without realizing it? Had I really made progress, or was I still stuck in my old ways and it just didn't seem obvious to me? I found it hard to believe that I wasn't meant to be a writer since it had been my dream for such a long time. I started looking at job boards and began applying to as many writing jobs as possible.

Weeks turned into months and I was getting nowhere in finding a new job. I wasn't even getting called in for interviews. With each passing day, I became more depressed, and that narrative of not being good enough was back.

I was telling myself that I wasn't a good writer after all, and that must have been why I wasn't getting hired. I was completely unsure of what else to turn to for my career. I felt like a complete failure, and what was worse was the realization that everything I had done to build my self-esteem I had allowed to be torn down all because I had been laid off. I had never felt so ashamed and was disappointed to have let myself down.

Almost six months after losing my job, and with a large weight of uncertainty on my shoulders, I began to seek solace and comfort at the yoga studio I had been going to on and off for many years. Being on my mat brought a sense of calm over me, and attending classes felt very therapeutic. Flowing through the yoga poses felt like flowing my troubles away. One evening after a class, the yoga instructor suggested one of their training programs to me after we had a conversation about what I had gone through and how I was feeling. I thought it was odd to take their 200-hour teacher training program since I had no desire to be a yoga teacher, but something she said to me clicked. She told me that while I may not go on to be a yoga instructor after getting the certification, doing the program might help me gain the clarity I was seeking in my life.

She explained how the program could help me deepen my yoga practice, get in touch with my spiritual side, and get in tune with my soul purpose. After reflecting on her words for about a week, I chose to sign up for the 200-hour yoga teacher training certification and began the program in September 2018. I had no idea that this decision would be a powerful pivoting moment in my life.

I was immersed in this program for six months, practicing yoga a few times a week, reading books and manuals based on the curriculum, and attending the monthly training sessions. Every month we would meet and train for 20 hours throughout one weekend. Those weekends were a bit intense, but it was all worth it.

What I was learning, the connections I was making, and the things that I was discovering about myself were remarkable. I had so many breakthroughs and "a-ha" moments during that time. What that yoga instructor had said to me just before I signed up was true. Not only was I deepening my yoga practice and growing to love all that yoga brings to my life, but I was also gaining clarity on what I truly wanted for myself. What I discovered surprised me and in the best way!

I completed my yoga teacher training just as I was reaching the one-year mark since being laid off. I started thinking that maybe the reason I was here, one year later and still no job, was because I had been on the wrong path all along. What became clear to me during my yoga teacher training was that I was meant to be doing something to serve others and that my purpose lay in helping people in some way. Could I accomplish that as a writer? Possibly. Though at that moment in time my gut was telling me to connect to my purpose through yoga. And that's exactly what I did.

I began looking into finding a space I could teach classes from and figuring out what I could call my business. In early 2019, *Mindful Yoga Moments* was born. I chose this name because through my teaching I wanted to encourage people to find mindful moments every day to practice self-care through yoga and meditation.

Working for myself was a completely foreign idea to me and I knew I would need help, so I also searched for someone who might be able to coach me through this process. By sheer fate, I ended up meeting online a woman named Maria Alexandra, who is a life and business coach based in Miami. I found Maria because an author I follow posted that she was going to be interviewed by her and I thought I would check out the interview. This led me to follow Maria and join her Facebook group, which in turn resulted in Maria and I chatting within her group, and then through private messages.

One day, as we were going back and forth chatting on Messenger, she asked if I would like to do a quick video call, and so we did. I opened up to Maria about what I had been through, where it had led me, and how I was looking for help starting this new venture as a yoga teacher. She told me about a new coaching program she was launching and asked me if I would be interested in working with her. Without hesitation, I said yes. The connection I felt with her was undeniable and I knew that this was the start of a beautiful journey.

Within a couple of months of that conversation, I began Maria's *Rock Your Life* mastermind coaching program. Through this program, I connected with seven incredible women who were all on a journey to finding their purpose and taking leaps of faith, just like I was. Together, we helped each other as we carved our path by supporting, listening, and cheering each other on. Despite thousands of kilometers separating us (our group had members living from the west coast of Canada to the shores of Florida and in between), and the fact that we only saw each other online, we became a close group of sisters, taking steps that brought us closer to rocking our lives! Every woman in that group inspired and motivated me, and helped me see that nothing is impossible. I had many moments of wanting to give up and they all encouraged me. These ladies constantly reminded me that I was worth fighting for and that I had something special to offer others. My months-long coaching journey with them showed me the power of women supporting women, which in turn helped me discover that empowering other women was part of my purpose.

One particularly poignant moment I experienced with these ladies came during our weekend retreat together. (Side note:

we ended our coaching journey by spending a weekend together in Florida. It was wonderful to be with my *Rock Your Life* sisters in person after months of just sharing our journey online). On our second night together, we went out to dinner and Maria led us in a beautiful activity right there in the restaurant.

We each brought our notebooks and pens with us, and we took turns sharing with each member the gifts we saw in them. When it was my turn, Maria grabbed my notebook and pen (this was done for all of us) and wrote down the list of gifts my sisters saw in me. Each of these amazing women took their turn saying "Jennifer, the gifts I see in you are…," and finished that sentence with the most wonderful words of empowerment.

It brought tears to my eyes. I finally had a positive list of words to describe me; words that I could now use in my narrative and replace with the old negative ones from my childhood. Even though I'd had other people over the years describe me in a positive light, I always just politely nodded and smiled, accepting the compliment but not truly believing it. This was the first time I could listen to being described positively and believe it. To this day, whenever I need some words of encouragement, I open that notebook and read that powerful list my dear friends wrote for me.

I finished the *Rock Your Life* mastermind coaching program at the end of 2019 and continued building my yoga teaching. I spent time setting some goals for the coming year of my business. I wanted to connect with students looking to deepen their yoga practice, as well as with other women, who, like me, struggled with their mental health and are looking for support. I made plans for teaching different types of yoga classes and hosting various workshops about mindfulness, meditation, and well-being. I began the process of networking with other local female entrepreneurs to form partnerships for the workshops I wanted to organize. I was so excited about what the new year would bring! Little did I know what exactly the year 2020 would bring to all of us.

When the coronavirus pandemic hit, I was met yet again with a lot of uncertainty, as were many other people. Not knowing the severity of what was happening in our world, I thought that it would be a temporary blip in my plan for my yoga business.

I held on to my goals and my hopes for what I wanted to do with *Mindful Yoga Moments*. I had come such a long way in my journey that I didn't want to give up. By the second lockdown my optimistic view of how this pandemic would affect my yoga teaching was wearing off, and I found myself in what I would describe as a mourning period. I was angry and sad that something I'd worked so hard for was again not happening the way I wanted it to. But after all of these years, with everything I had been through and everything I had learned,

I saw myself handling this life experience differently than before. In the past, whenever I met a roadblock, I would break down, give up, and proclaim myself a failure. This time, I showed myself compassion, allowed myself to feel my emotions, and let go of what I couldn't control. Most importantly, I encouraged myself to move on. I had fallen many times before, and I was going to pick myself up once again. I'm still teaching yoga part-time and figuring out what the future holds for my business, but for once in my life, I am comfortable with the uncertainty.

Having to put my yoga business temporarily on hold while waiting through the pandemic lockdowns in Ontario allowed me to discover other options for using my skills and sharing my talents. In a moment of clarity, I began helping others by working as a virtual assistant and quickly decided to start another business in the spring of 2021. Part of me feels like I made this decision hastily, but to be honest, I feel so incredibly confident doing so. Working as a virtual assistant has allowed me to get back into writing and editing again on a regular basis, as well as tap into my creativity more with image designs that I do for social media. Plus, I've had the bonus of working with some amazing female entrepreneurs and business owners. As I venture into this new line of entrepreneurship, I feel stronger than I ever have!

I feel like I have found the perfect balance with these two businesses I have chosen to embark on – using my spiritual side to help others through yoga and meditation, and using my creative and practical skills to support small business owners. I finally feel like I've found my true purpose.

An important lesson that I've learned on my journey is that the mindset we choose plays a key role in living a happy life. We have two choices: we can either dwell on the negative and let that be our driving force as we live out our days, or, we can try to see the positive, even during challenging times, and ultimately live a life with more joy. Although it took me a long time to figure this out, I have chosen to see more lightness than darkness in my life.

I have learned how to catch myself when I'm narrowing in on the bad and make the choice to change my train of thought to something good.

I have learned to see failure in a different light. I accept the fact that we all fail sometimes, and that failing or making mistakes doesn't make me stupid, worthless, or not good enough. I see the value now in recognizing my mistakes and learning from them. My failures are like my battle scars, each one reminding me of how the lesson I learned from them made me stronger. I came across a social media post once that I think sums this up perfectly – I am flaw some! (Defined as a person who embraces their flaws and mistakes but knows that they are awesome anyway!)

This leads me to the biggest obstacle I've had to overcome along this path...learning to love myself. I have to admit that this is a work in progress, as I still have moments when I can be hard on myself and instantly criticize rather than show myself compassion, but boy, have I come a long way in this aspect of my life. I have made a deeper connection to my spiritual side and feel more grounded. I have learned to trust my intuition and to show myself grace and compassion. I have learned to recognize my good qualities, embrace them, and best of all, celebrate them.

I think the greatest part of my journey is realizing how far I've come, recognizing how much I've learned, and acknowledging that even the moments I had considered to be failures were experiences that helped shape who I am today. I can't look at my past mistakes with regret. I can only look at them with gratitude for what they've taught me. When I reflect on the girl I once was and the woman I am now, I can look at her with love in my heart, and feel proud for never giving up on her.

Dedication

To my husband, Paul: Thank you for always being there for me and loving me unconditionally. Your support has given me the courage to pursue my dreams and the strength to embark on a journey of healing and self-love. I am grateful and blessed to have you by my side.

To my son, Ben, and my daughter, Charlotte: You may not realize it, but you both motivate me every day to be a better woman and mother. I strive to be a great role model for you, by teaching you to never give up on yourself and to be kind, compassionate, and loving individuals. Thank you for being such amazing kids!

To my parents, Raquel and Tony: Through every bump in my journey, you both have been there no matter what, often dropping everything just to support and help me. I am so blessed to be your daughter and love you both so much.

To my brother, Chris: Over 3,000 km separates us but you're always close to my heart. I'm grateful to have you as my big brother and know you're always there if I need you.

To the rest of my family, my friends, and all the amazing people I have met on my journey who have encouraged and empowered me – I am forever thankful!

Much love, *Jennifer*

My family photo credit Cheryl Bailey

My Husband (my rock) and I

Photo credit Cheryl Bailey

Photographer Cheryl Bailey

The universe has
shaken you
to
awaken you.

Fragments of Victoria's Empowerment Journey

By Victoria Trinh

I hate to say that my story is a tragic one, though I can at least say that through all the hardship I have come out as a stronger woman. Most of the memories of my childhood weren't the fondest. I guess we can start at the beginning. My parents are victims of being born into war. Unfortunately, the war stuck with them in our family home growing up, as my mother faced severe post-traumatic stress disorder (PTSD). I have survived watching my mother try to commit suicide from the age of five up until, well, now, as I still deal with it. Yet, just because I have been through so much doesn't mean I haven't started taking off the mask that I've used as a shield for so long.

It's safe to say that I have been through a lot in my life so far. From a physically, emotionally, and psychologically abusive upbringing to multiple horrible events, such as rape, shaming, and being homeless, to having my first child be murdered from within me.

Not all of my memories are horrible but the bad ones outweigh the good. I learned to survive the only way I could and became attention-seeking. I think my best years were when I lived with my grandma. She used to call me 小白兔口 (sew bak toe), meaning little white rabbit because I was born the year of a rabbit in May 1987 on Victoria Day. This is how I got my name. I surprised everyone as I was supposed to be a boy, according to my parents.

There were some times from my childhood when I remember my mom smiling, but not so much anymore. My mother was heartbroken when we accidentally told our teachers we were getting spanked as a form of discipline at home. I remember that was the first time I saw my mother try to commit suicide. I was only five years old, and I can recall hiding from the police in the upstairs closet with my brother telling me to stay quiet. After that, I witnessed her try to take her life multiple times more as a last resort anytime we didn't see eye to eye. I'm not sure what it was like for my brother but I have the memories that I wish I could forget or let go.

The good memories I have from growing up are of modelling and acting. My mom made sure things were fair so "if one sibling was doing something then the other sibling gets equal." I'm younger than my brother by six years, so naturally, my older brother set the standard most of the time.

My mom used to take me and my brother to a lot of casting calls, as well as piano lessons. Getting into acting was always more of my brother's thing. It wasn't until I was about 12 years old when my mom entered me into a contest for "cameo models" that I learned my mom was a former model back home before she had her life taken away from her due to the Vietnam War.

I went through a battle of survival before modelling became a better outlet for the pain and anger that I had for the world. As I mentioned earlier, I was shamed, bullied, and raped, all of which happened during my high school years. I was raped after school hours on the school stage. I can still remember the cold metal bars on the scaffold where he pinned me down, pushed my kilt up, and forcefully rammed his penis between my legs. I remember him covering one hand over my mouth, while that same hand and arm bared all his weight on me to keep me quiet. His other hand bruised my thighs. I didn't fight back. My body went numb.

You're probably wondering how we got access to the school stage after hours. I have to admit that I was a bit of a nerd. I was a techie and part of the stage crew in school. I've always loved being on stage and behind the scenes. I liked knowing the process from start to finish of production. I've always had an eye for beautiful things. I was also part of the art council and played tennis.

Fast forward to making a fresh, new start. I moved to a new city and new school but ended up being homeless in the dead of winter for almost six to eight months. Man, oh man, did I learn a lot of street smarts back then. I met some pretty amazing people who I still call my chosen sisters today. One, in particular, took me in on really cold snowstorms and helped me stay in school until my family found out I was kicked out under false pretenses. It was then that I was forced to drop out of art school and get into dental school.

Things started to look up a little for me, or so I thought. I became engaged but unfortunately, my ex-fiancé was very abusive. It was through this relationship that I found my voice. I may have lost my faith in God, as my grandmother passed away during this time, but I did find my voice. I no longer spoke like a mouse. I no longer spoke in my throat and I began talking back more. I had watched all the family who put me down and continue to put me down all these years, be able to live their lives and I kept thinking to myself: *When is it my turn? When do I get to treat myself as number one and not trash begging at everyone else's feet?* This was when I decided to start modelling more seriously.

I started with boudoir modelling and swimwear, then later moved into fashion, cosplay and creatives, and bridal modelling. My current goal is to do more bridal, runway fashion, and focus on being published.

My family was not behind me on this decision. By this time, I had fought for my life with a very abusive ex-fiancé, and went back to school again, only to drop out of nursing to continue in dental. This is where I found my home for the next eight years and when I started international modelling part-time.

For me, modelling is my lifeline, my healthy, but expensive, hobby-turned career. It is a source of creative and emotional outlet and a way to verbally speak my words without really speaking at all.

As my journey started to take a more positive turn, I found myself once again in a bad relationship. It was the beginning of the Covid-19 pandemic and he was just as bad as my ex-fiancé, if not worse, yet this time I ended up pregnant. In a flash my heart filled with joy, then quickly was overcome by intense fear. I was foolish to turn a blind eye to every single red flag that he had. I was right to be fearful. I fought him with everything in my body to try and protect our baby, but he forced me to have an abortion against my will and without my knowledge. From that point onward, all the hard therapy work I had done my whole life was out the window. I began to see myself as a failure of the worst kind. I wasn't even able to

111

shower unless I was fully clothed because I could not look at my naked body. Anyone who knows me knows how badly I wanted to be a young mother. My dream was to have a family and be a mother by my mid-20's, but I was told because of certain health conditions it might be hard to carry full-term or even get pregnant at all the older I become. So, you can understand why I was beside myself when my child was murdered from within me. Still, I tried to slowly pick myself up and not let the loss of my baby turn me into a negative person.

Months later, I ended up going to see a Vincent Van Gogh gallery (side note, this is one of my favorite artists). It was here that I met Danny Smith, an artist that I have admired for many years. He was very sweet with his words and the way he treated me – like a normal person and not as a 'model' – is when I began to find confidence in myself again. It was surprising to me how his kind words of encouragement to get out of bed and friendly chats helped me find a silver lining, as well as begin to believe in God again. I felt as though my Angel baby was helping both me and my ex find happiness within ourselves again. Danny also helped me love my body again and start modelling a more natural version of me. I became more body-positive. My pregnancy gave me more curves and I embraced them.

I am very fortunate to have the support group that I do as I go through these hard times, as well as a partner who supports me wholeheartedly. I'm grateful for connecting with *SuzyQJewels* and the warm welcome and support Suzy and her team have provided me over the years as well.

Each day is a work in progress for me. I'm now trying to go back to school in health care so I can have a better future, but I won't be slowing down with my modelling any time soon. I still go to therapy regularly, and I continue to promote women's empowerment through my daily activities and with each photoshoot or set that I'm on.

Dedication

I dedicate this story to my late grandma, Xám, and my lover for always being patient and lovingly supportive of me.

Portrait March 2020 by JESSICA CHIN KING Makeup by Binny Makeup Artist Location Toronto, Ont @jessica.chin.king @binny_makeup

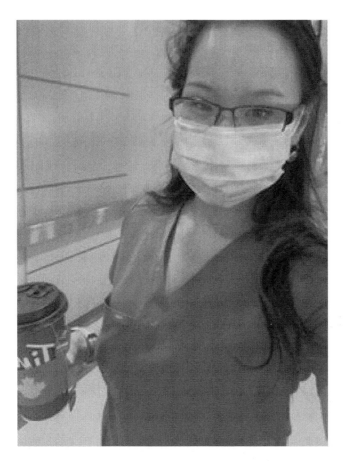

Healing Postpartum Boudoir Session with Joshua Clifford
November 2021, Makeup Artist Self
Location Hamilton, On
@sensiblesensual_photo
@bigred_photography

Asian Fashion Week Runway Show for Suzy Tamasy
July 2018? Photographer David Fillion Productions
Toronto, Ont @davidfillion

Promo Swimwear for Cupshe Swimwear
Summer 2020-2021 Photographer Mike Streeter
Mississauga, Ontario @mikestreeterphoto

first Hamilton Fashion Week for Ken and Kristal Beinier
Hamilton, Ontario summer year 2016-2019 @hamfashionweek

behind the scenes with Makeup artist Binny summer 2021
Toronto,ON @binny_makeup

The Misfit

By Sadia Salauddin

When I was asked to write this story, I didn't know where to start. To be honest, I was quite surprised. What could I ever say to empower another person, let alone other women? In my opinion, women can be the hardest people to inspire, being another woman myself. We can sometimes be mean, judgemental, ready to tear each other apart given the slightest chance. Haven't we all been there? I know I have. I guess I have come a long way from that awkward, dark-skinned, tomboy kid I used to be and a part of me has always connected with the so-called 'misfits.' Therefore, I feel compelled to tell a story. One of truth, of a journey, and of life.

Although I was born in Chittagong, Bangladesh, I grew up a part of my younger childhood in the Middle East. My father accepted a job in Abu Dhabi shortly after I was born and we moved there as a family. After three years, we were blessed with my younger sister, and my father got posted to Saudi

Arabia. We happily spent several years in Saudi Arabia living everywhere from Al-Khobar to Jeddah, basically anywhere my

dad got posted. Due to the nature of my father's work, as a mechanical engineer, his postings would be at remote sites with no decent schooling nearby. Therefore, my mother, along with my sister and I, moved back to Bangladesh, our homeland. This time we decided on the capital, Dhaka, as it was a booming economy at the time and most of our relatives from both sides of the family lived there.

This was a huge culture shock for a young girl who had never really known her homeland and had already been schooled up to the third grade, at an American school, in the Middle East. We were enrolled in the best English medium school in the capital.

I was forced to start from grade one because, although I spoke it, I did not know how to read or write in Bengali, my mother tongue. My American accent didn't add to the easing into the school process either. I was immediately teased and deemed an outsider by most of my classmates. To add to the situation, I was a tomboy and had enjoyed spending long, happy hours playing and swimming under the Middle Eastern sun. I had inherited none of my mother's milky white fair genes or the shy manner of most Bengali girls. Just to clarify, dark skin is considered to be ugly in my culture. From a young age, I was teased and bullied, mostly by the so-called 'in' crowd girls, for not being fairer and more lady-like, basically, more like them. But I was never the type to be swayed by such people. My father raised me like a son and I was a headstrong tomboy from a very young age. Blessed by an amazing friend circle throughout my school life and the constant love and support of my family, I led the happy existence of a teenager engrossed in my life with family, friends, studies, and sports. I always knew I had bigger things to do in life. During my final years of schooling, my father, who still worked in the Middle East at the time, applied for immigration to Canada. As soon as I graduated, we moved as a family to start a new beginning.

Even though it was a big move, we were no stranger to living abroad and welcomed this change as a fantastic new opportunity. We initially moved to Ottawa and stayed with relatives there. I immediately was enrolled in the university there in the Business Administration program which I looked forward to starting. We moved when my father bought a house. During my time at the university in Ottawa, I made a lot of friends, many from countries I had only ever heard or read of. The multi-culturalism in Canada is something I truly appreciated then and have grown to love now that I call it my home. Although I had friends in school, a part of me felt lonely for my close childhood friends who were studying in the USA at the time. I was delighted to know that a few good friends from Bangladesh had decided to come study in Toronto.

This began my journey to falling in love with the amazing 'T-Dot,' one of the many names it is so fondly known and called by locals.

My friends were international students and were staying at a university campus in north Toronto. I would often drive down to visit on the weekends and loved the ambiance and the hustle and bustle of a big city. Ottawa, despite being the capital, was not only smaller in population, but also much quieter. I decided I wanted to move and transferred to a university in downtown Toronto. I was able to transfer my credits and enrolled in Business Management. I graduated with a Bachelor of Commerce degree in Marketing Management and Communications. It was during this time that I delved into modelling as a hobby. What began as a small, fun segment of a South Asian event on campus led to 15+ years of modelling on and off. During this time, I have been featured on many of the biggest Canadian runways to numerous magazine features and covers. Who would have imagined that an awkward, insecure tomboy from Bangladesh would ever be a model? I certainly never did.

For anyone entering the modelling industry, I highly recommend having some good profile and portfolio pictures taken to display some basic work. This is always what is asked from models anytime they are applying for any jobs, whether it's agency or freelance. Many photographers out there are just starting in the industry and would happily take pictures for a cheap rate or if you are lucky, even for free, so they can add them to their portfolio and social media. Networking is also very important. These days it is very easy to find modelling groups on social media or posts for runway shows and model audition calls. Talk to other models; reach out to local designers, etc. The more people you know in the industry, the more you will likely connect with the right ones. Most of all, you need to have thick skin because the entertainment industry can be cutthroat and mean. Never let it get to you, and if this is what you are serious about, never quit.

Still, this was something I only ever considered a hobby and not a career. I always wanted more mental stimulation, a challenge, and to be able to give back to the city that gave me so much.

I was blessed to have worked in many different environments right after graduation. From face-to-face customer service at a downtown Toronto mall to large corporate office settings. Even though initially not all were anywhere near the ideal career that I wanted, they, nonetheless, taught me a lot of necessary life skills. I worked part-time, contracts, temp, and full-time jobs and have had my share of financial and personal struggles. From minimum wage to getting fired, I have seen it all, and all of these experiences shaped me into who I am today.

I am now the Assistant Director of Admissions for the online division for a prominent college that happens to be Canada's largest post-secondary institution with campuses from coast to coast. I have always wanted to make a difference, especially in the life of the younger generation, and there is no better way than through education. It may have taken time but I am proud of how far I have come. Never give up on your goals, dreams, and ambitions. No matter where you are from, what you have been through, or what people say or think you are, stayed focused, stay real and true to yourself, work hard, and be disciplined. You are strong, you are brave, and you can do it! Never let anyone tell you otherwise. One love.

Dedication

In loving dedication to my amazing parents, Yusuf and Rosie. Thank you for always letting me spread my wings and fly.

At a photoshoot wearing SQJ Published

Bella in the Forest wearing SQJ published.

Photographer Cheryl Bailey at Divas in Durham Fundraiser

Photographer RB wearing SQJ in Toronto Published

LOVE IS PATIENT, LOVE IS KIND.
IT DOES NOT ENVY, IT DOES NOT BOAST, IT IS NOT PROUD.
IT IS NOT RUDE, IT IS NOT SELF-SEEKING,
IT IS NOT EASILY ANGERED, IT KEEPS NO
RECORD OF WRONGS. LOVE DOES NOT DELIGHT IN
EVIL, BUT REJOICES WITH THE TRUTH.
IT ALWAYS PROTECTS, ALWAYS TRUSTS,
ALWAYS HOPES, ALWAYS PERSEVERES.

LOVE NEVER FAILS.

- 1 CORINTHIANS 13:4-8 -

Finding My Worth

By Kimberly Anne Cranley

I always had a feeling that I was made for greatness, but it took an uphill journey to *really* figure it out, and I'm currently still climbing.

Growing up, it was just me and my mom for the first part of my life. My birth father abandoned us when I was a little girl; he was an abusive alcoholic so it was probably for the best (actually, I think I can say it was definitely for the best). I can see this now as an adult but as a kid, I was hurt and confused: How does a father walk away from his own daughter? I remember sitting in my little yellow chair staring out the window waiting for him to come to get me. Sometimes he showed up drunk, while other times he showed up hours late until eventually, he didn't show up at all.

My mom and I lived in an apartment building. She did her best to support us but we were barely getting by. She worked full-time and put herself through night school to try to create a better life for us.

This story will repeat itself later on …

One day, I met this man who lived next door. Being a young girl of about four or five years old at the time, and with no stable father figure, I was looking for fatherly love. He was a kind man whom I liked right away and he was always outside working on his truck. I would go and see him when he was out there in the parking lot working away and he would teach me how to change the oil and check the fluids. We would spend hours together out there shining up his black Silverado.

The day he invited me and my mom over for my favourite dinner, which was spaghetti and meat sauce, was a day that would change all our lives.

It led to us all moving out of that dumpy apartment and moving into a house together, followed by him and my mom getting married. I finally had the dad that I longed for since my early childhood years. The best part was that his name was Kim, too, so we had the same name. He would tell people he named me after him.

Growing up, I had two amazing parents. They ended up getting married and buying a house in the south end of Oshawa. We were your typical middle-class family with both my parents working hard to make ends meet. My mom had a corporate 9 to 5 job and my dad worked shifts at General Motors. I found myself alone a lot longing for a big happy family like the ones you would see on TV.

I was about eight years old when I remember being bullied for the first time. Looking back, if I had been diagnosed, the doctors would have said social anxiety. I think I still have it to this day, but I'm no doctor and you would never know it because I've learned to hide it well.

I remember the anxiety of walking to school and wondering if it would be a good day. I would try to think of something funny to say, but it was always the same thing: I was bullied and made fun of for all kinds of reasons, one of them being the way I looked. The mole above my lip was a great target for kids. I remember my mom telling me it made me special and unique. She would tell me all of that amazing stuff moms say, but I just wanted to be like everyone else. I swore one day I would get it removed. I tried so hard to fit in and never wanted to stand out.

By the time high school came, the area we lived in had become pretty rough so my parents decided to move me up to a small town called Little Britain (if you don't know where that is, that's okay as most people don't). It's a small "if you blink, you'll miss it" kind of town.

I was 15 years old and in the second half of grade nine at this point, which made the move very difficult for me. I was hopeful for a fresh start somewhere nobody knew me. I thought I could change my story from a loser to a cool new kid.

The first day in my new high school everyone was so different from what I was used to. They all had their cliques and once again I did not fit in. I was the city kid who was uprooted and dropped down in the middle of a field where everyone was wearing plaid and overalls, and then there was me in tight jeans and tummy tops. I stood out like a sore thumb and found myself as the perfect target for bullies. Yep, they loved me.

I was alone and rebellious. The friends that I did end up making in Oshawa were all left behind me an hour and a half away and I felt alone in the world again. So, I did what any teenager would do: I got mixed up in a bad crowd and started to ruin my life. Drugs and alcohol were the name of the game and skipping school was cool. I was headed down a bad path, fast. I found that I finally fit in and my social anxiety would go away when the drugs and alcohol were in my system. By grade 11, I had completely dropped out, moved out of my parents' house, and was couch hopping. If you would have seen me then you would have figured I was headed for rehab and jail. This went on for most of my teen years, and I became the party girl that would do anything once.

In my early 20s, I found myself searching for love in all the wrong places with no self-love or boundaries and really no idea of what I deserved. I was quick to fall for the "bad boy" – bar fights and tattoos were where it was at. We were young, crazy, and free! We would spend our nights dancing and drinking with a splash of drugs, and then our days were spent fighting over the nights. The relationship was the furthest from healthy, but then again, so were we. What came next was what would change everything, and man did I ever need a change...I just didn't know it.

I found myself pregnant at 21 years old; it was time to grow up! Living in a barn apartment with my boyfriend and a roommate and finding out I'm pregnant is not the situation every girl dreamed of. It's more like the situation every mother is afraid of. With no high school diploma and only bartending experience, I was not fit to be a mom. I could hardly take care of myself, to be honest. None of that matters when you are pregnant; it was time to get my shit together and I only had nine months and 50% normal energy to do it. So, that's what we did. We tried to go from wild crazy party animals to mom and dad pretty much overnight.

My dad found us a little farmhouse to rent, we moved out of our party house, and my boyfriend got down on one knee. We had an instant family and we were getting married. It was going to be like those TV families I had watched in my younger years and dreamed of being a part of until reality smacked us both right in the face. You need a strong foundation to build your dreams and we had no foundation at all. Everything happened so fast and change at high speed is not sustainable change. Just like building a business or losing weight, doing things slow and steady is best so it doesn't all crumble. But when it's built too fast? Well, our instant family lasted a couple of years before it ended in a tragic split.

I became a single mom. History was repeating itself, just like my mom had experienced with me. Abuse and alcohol eventually led to my daughter's father walking away and leaving me a single mom on welfare struggling to survive. Food banks...I've been there. Not having a cent to my name and no food in the fridge – I've experienced that, as well as the reality of going without so my daughter could eat. I was judged by family and friends, as none of them were really surprised I ended up where I did. This was my rock bottom. What surprised them is what happened next!

I knew I couldn't stay there and that I needed a plan. I started working on myself. I found myself in a Catholic Church but they told me I was not welcome there (true story). My life was such a mess I thought God didn't even love me.

This made me look within. I started reading Louise Hay's books, began learning to love myself, and realized that my past didn't have to equal my future. I found the law of attraction and watched the movie *The Secret*. I went to the library and read personal development books. This helped me to feel like I could believe again. I remember driving around the middle-class parts of my city dreaming of living there. I would pull into a driveway to turn around, but for a second, I would pretend it was my house, that my amazing family was inside, and I was coming home. I would do this in my free time and I really enjoyed it. It may seem crazy, but it gave me hope.

I ended up getting a corporate job as a project manager's assistant at an engineering firm. Doing 10 to life at a 9 to 5 job, making an hourly wage, and getting benefits for me and my daughter. It was boring for me but this was the way I was supposed to be. Even though it felt more like a life sentence, I was able to rent one of those houses in the middle-class area. I got off the system and out of housing. I was stronger than ever before. I was proud of myself and independent. The storm had ended and bright days were ahead.

About six months later, I met my future husband, Shaun. I knew from our first date he was the one. You see, I had created a must-have list and I was not willing to settle after everything I had been through. I had just gotten back on my feet and I wasn't about to repeat the same mistakes. I didn't *need* a man, but I wanted to have a great guy in my life and I wasn't about to stop until I found him. I used what I learned from my past relationship to create a list of must-haves and found that I had become very picky! I had things on this list like must NOT play video games, must be six feet or taller, must be stable in his profession, and so on. I had also set rules of how I expected to be treated and set boundaries; I used lists to remind myself. I promised myself that if they broke even one of my boundaries that was a red flag and I was out! Shortly after starting to date again, I met Shaun, and the minute he hugged me I felt like I was home. I think it was the longest first hug of my life. Neither of us wanted to let go. He checked every box on my must-have list. I was blown away because I even thought I was asking for too much.

As time went on, he continued to exceed my expectations and ended up teaching me how I am meant to be treated. I can't forget this one day we were out for dinner at our favourite restaurant and we both ordered the same thing. When our meals showed up, Shaun told the waiter to give me the bigger steak. I was shocked. We both knew I couldn't eat it all and he is much bigger than me. When I asked him why he gave me the bigger steak, Shaun said it was because he will always make sure that I have more than enough, that a man puts a woman's needs before his own, and that this was how our relationship would be. It's been 10 years now and he has taught me so much. Shaun ended up adopting my daughter, signing up to raise another man's child emotionally, physically, and financially; he promised to always be there for Mariah. Shortly after that, we got married and together we bought our first house. I became pregnant with our second daughter and since I had a corporate job, I was able to go on maternity leave.

Life wasn't all sunshine and rainbows though. My parents were separating and my dad was having health problems. He had fallen down the stairs and hurt his knee. He went through operation after operation, with the doctor butchering his knee and leaving him addicted to pain meds and unable to get out of bed. The night I found out I was pregnant my dad went to jail. I tell you this because life is not easy; even in some of the best moments, you are fighting other battles. I have learned to focus on the positive and to see what is in my control, which are my actions and attitude. So often we want to save people from their journey instead of focusing on our own.

After my parents split and things levelled out, my dad moved five hours away to be with his family and my mom sold the house and rented a little cottage on the lake. I had my second daughter, Rylynn Alita Cranley, in September 2014 and I finally had a family of my own. It was something I had always dreamed of... and then the next plot twist happened.

About five months after having Rylynn, we found out I was pregnant again. This was not our plan but God/the universe works in mysterious ways. Cali Grace would change everything, and she actually saved me from the corporate rat race.

After having just bought a house and cars, even with two incomes, my maternity leave would only pay for 12 months. I wasn't going to be able to go back to work because we quickly went from having one child to three kids to support. My past trauma of not being able to support my daughter was hitting me hard and I ended up with anxiety and depression. I remember praying for a way out and praying to God saying, "Please have a plan for me. Please don't let me go back to struggling to survive." I think I prayed every day, all day in my head while crying. We went into survival mode looking to save money wherever we could.

We cut our cable and found this cool invention called an Android box. Shortly after getting it our friends would come over just to see what was going on with our TV. All our friends wanted one and this is when I decided to go into business for myself. I spoke with the company that made them and they were happy to have me selling them. They would give me a cut on everything I sold. It was about $1,000 to get started but I knew the demand was there and I would make my money back quickly if I hustled.

I started inviting everyone I knew over to show them these devices and by the time I had Cali, I had replaced my income working from home. I had grown a sales team of around 40 reps and was holding demos every Saturday and Sunday from 1-2 in my living room while my babies napped.
Rylynn and Cali are 14 months and one day apart and while they were a handful, business was booming. I was able to get a

nanny to help with the girls while I crushed my business. Things were starting to look up. We were coming into the Christmas season, our first Christmas with our three girls, and I felt confident that we could provide and give our daughters the best first family Christmas.

One night late that December, I got a call from the people manufacturing the boxes. They informed me that they were being sued by the big cable companies and they had to shut the operation down immediately. This meant I had to call all of my salespeople and lay them off right before Christmas. This also meant that the money I was counting on to pay my bills, mortgage, and buy Christmas presents was all gone. Shaun and I had built a bit of savings but I knew it wasn't going to last as long. I was crushed by the fear I knew so well: *Here we go again*, I thought to myself, *I knew it was too good to be true.*

I spent my days in tears and my nights lying awake for a couple of months and then I got a call from my business partner. She had a new opportunity she wanted to chat about. One day in March, she came over and showed me this online business she swore she saw great potential in. I was desperate as we were quickly running out of savings. It was $1,000 to join and that was all I had left in my account. I gave her my money and went all in like my life depended on it.

A few days later, some boxes of household cleaning products showed up at my door and I had no idea what to do with them. I opened them up, smelled them, and put them in my back room before I called up my business partner and begged for a refund. It wasn't that they weren't good products. I thought they smelled amazing; like they were scented with natural oils instead of perfume. I believed that these products were exactly what people were looking for but I didn't know how to run an online business or truly believed you could make money online.

Desperation can make you do dumb things. Thank goodness she didn't give me the refund that I begged for and instead she taught me about attraction marketing and showed me a selling system that worked. Soon, all my family and friends were hooked on these products and things were going well.

Then one day, my dad called me and he sounded worried. As we chatted about life, he told me that he was always going to be there for me and that if I was in trouble, I could turn to him. I asked what prompted him to say that and he admitted to me that he was worried about me and the work I was doing. He was worried that it was a cult and that they would take all my money (he must not have known that we were struggling financially). I reassured him that I was making money by sending him my first $100 paycheque, but that conversation with my dad honestly hurt deeply. I remember all these feelings setting in, and wondering who was talking about me, what were they saying, and were people laughing at me behind my back? All of these thoughts put a halt to the business that I was starting to grow online.

I found myself struggling more with depression and anxiety and began questioning if it was time to go to the doctor and get some medication. I had everything I've ever wanted: an amazing husband, my own business, a house, and three beautiful girls. My life was complete but I still wasn't happy. I started to do some research, which led me to become fascinated with health and wellness. I began to work out and eat healthily, and soon saw a dramatic change in my mental health. By this point, my online company came out with a weight-loss program that my husband and I both tried. The supplements were clean and natural and helped with boosting focus, health, and vitality. We both saw amazing changes in three months. I went from a size 12 to a size 5 and my husband lost over 20 pounds. We were feeling great by working out and eating right and the people around us could see that. My business was booming and once again things were on the upswing.

From there, things expanded quickly with new partners and customers. It was almost like overnight I became a leader but I felt like I was less than qualified. I knew the leader I wanted to be but I just hadn't arrived there yet. I remember talking to a mentor and him telling me that this is a personal development business with a comp plan, so I started to learn about how my brain works and how to rewire it. I observed my triggers and my reactions. I stopped blaming others and forced myself to look at how I responded. It was no easy task with the past I had and the triggers that were deeply rooted in my soul from childhood. I had a lot of work to do. As I'm writing this, I'm still working on myself and that work will never stop. I can honestly say I'm finally growing into the leader that I've always wanted to be. It's taken five long hard years but I'm proud of who I'm becoming. I've gone through so much pain to get to where I am today, but I believe the pain we experience prompts us to change and grow.

Three years into my business I hit one of the top ranks in the company called 'Elite.' They say only one percent of people achieve this in online marketing, but I don't believe that. I truly believe that anyone can do it. I mean, I went from being a single mom, living on welfare with no education; I had a whole lot of reasons not to succeed. Now, I have a global team and work with some of the best leaders. Money is no longer an issue and business is thriving. I believe online businesses are the new way of the world. By saying yes to this opportunity, my life has changed forever and I've become a better and healthier person, both physically and mentally. I have helped so many others change their lives too! I love my life every day! I live in a beautiful house on the lake and run a globe business all from my phone. This is what fuels my passion. Do I work hard? Absolutely! I jump out of bed every morning excited for the day and to continue to build my dreams!

I'm so honoured I get to share my story with you. I hope that you will think of me when the plot twists happen in your life and you remember that no matter how bad it gets, you are one decision away from changing your life. I believe that where attention goes, energy flows, so focus on the positive and let the negative work itself out.

Dedication

This is dedicated to the men in my life who stood up when other men didn't: In memory of my dad, Kim Hansen, who raised me as his own, as well as to my incredible husband, Shaun Cranley. To my mother, Mary Hansen, for teaching me how to be a strong woman. I also want to dedicate this to my three beautiful daughters; may they always reach for the stars and never settle. Lastly, but definitely not least, I want to dedicate this to my team and customers because without them I wouldn't be where I am today and none of this would be worth it. We aren't here to do this life alone and I'm grateful for those who surround me.

143

From False Security to Total Freedom

By Beverley Thomson

At the age of five, I was cleaning my gramma's cupboards to get a stick of Juicy Fruit gum or a decadent maraschino cherry chocolate. My grandparents were the only stable parents I knew growing up since I had hippie parents from the opposite side of the tracks. My mom was a born-again Christian and my dad was a fun-loving alcoholic who knew how to enjoy life. Both of my parents and my grandparents inspired me in different ways; my mom in a spiritual way, my dad in a physical way, and my grandparents in a mentally stable way.

At my earliest age, I remember my mom shaking me at night because she was happy my dad was on his way home. I was her assurance that dad would come home from the bar to his little girl. I think that was the beginning of me experiencing anxiety attacks. My dad loved his little girl. My mom would dress me up and await his arrival. When I started kindergarten, I woke up at 5 a.m. to prepare myself mentally to walk to school on my own and attend class. I was so frightened and didn't want to leave my parents. I remember hearing my parents fighting about my dad's infidelities and feeling so scared because I didn't want my father to leave home. How would I ever survive without him?

My dad was an entrepreneur and inventor. He was always coming up with the next big idea. Sometimes we were rich with cars and maids, and other times we lived in churches or with friends. Meanwhile, I was shuffled off to be with my grandparents while my parents figured things out. At times my mom tried to do it on her own, but my grandmother always said "she made her bed and now must lie in it," so my mom always took my dad back and we were always moving, never living in one place longer than a year.

My teenage years were spent living in Owen Sound, Ontario. It was a fun time in my life. I had a religious boyfriend, then a rock and roll boyfriend, and I found jobs working in local pizza parlors. My mom always made me go to church while living under her roof. This interfered with my social life. One day, she saw me smoking downtown, pulled the cigarette out of my mouth, dragged me by my long hair into the car, and took a wooden spoon to me when I got home. This was not going to work out for either of us. I thought my mom was mean, strict, and quiet. I wanted to be like my dad and enjoy life.

I will never forget the day I came home after school to learn my mom had sent my dad packing and she turned my stray dog over to the Humane Society. I was devastated, hurt, and angry and I wanted to leave my home as soon as possible. I loved that dog! His name was Buddy and he was my best friend. My father and my dog were gone and my mom provided no reason for why it happened. No discussion, no answers, just gone. As time went on, my mom wanted to move on with her life and remarry, and I was in the way. My brother went to live with my mom's best friend, Reha. I had two choices: marry into a religious family with life on a farm, or leave home and find my own way in life. I choose the latter. I dropped out of school, packed my bags, and hit the road.

I decided to live with my rock and roller boyfriend's mom in Toronto and put myself through hair-dressing school while working nights as a bartender, even though I was underage. The girls at the school were different. They were classy but cliquish, and I felt like an outsider. Everyone's parents were paying for their school and I was paying for my own by working nights and weekends. The girls were so pretty and had beautiful clothes. I couldn't afford to wear brand-name clothes and jewellery. I wondered what it would be like and dreamed of having rich parents, but it just wasn't in my cards. I finally did bond with one girl who would steal at lunchtime from a local store. Her stealing caused me to become more anxious at school, but I was not going to rat her out since she was my only friend and could beat me up if she chose to. I was an outcast for some reason and to this day I don't understand why. Although my hairdressing teacher failed me and I had to stay extra months at school, I eventually passed and I was able to leave to become a hairdresser!

I tried working at many salons but continued to get fired. At one salon, an RCMP officer came in and asked me for a haircut. It was my first time doing such a short haircut, and the scissors seemed to take on their own life, creating bald spots all over his head when I tried to fix it. I soon found myself looking for a new job.

I met a new friend named Richard and we decided to have some fun. Since I wanted to find my father, I took Richard to hitchhike across Canada on a journey to find my dad. I worked as a hairdresser along the way, continued to get fired, but we made enough to buy food for us and our little dog.

When we reached Calgary, I was finally reunited with my long-lost dad. He was anything but rich and loved to drink. I ended up learning that Richard and my dad were both alcoholics. Richard became more and more aggressive as he drank and my dad suggested that I leave him. I wanted to, but I thought I loved Richard, so I stayed. When he started to blackout and beat me harder each night, I realized I was following in my mother's footsteps. My childhood anxiety was back and I was so afraid and ready to leave, but by morning Richard was normal again and such a kind, loving boyfriend. It was hard to fathom someone could change into two people. Finally, I got the courage to leave both my dad and Richard and headed back to Toronto to start a new life with my dog.

I was back in Toronto, living in a church basement with my dog. How did I end up back here with nothing again? I tried many jobs, from waitressing to hairdressing, but I either got fired for having my dog in my pocket or dropping something on a customer or just feeling out of it and unconscious. I felt numb, frozen, and scared but still needed to go on no matter how I felt. I lived in awful places, in dingy rooms with my tiny chihuahua that barked at the cockroaches crawling up the walls. It was hard to save enough money to get the first and last month's rent for my own place.

One day, hungry and needing to feed me and my dog, I went to a church and asked for help. They said I was not dressed properly and turned me away. Sitting in the park feeling sorry for myself, I found a free newspaper on a park bench. While reading through it, I found a job at a barbershop close by, so I decided to walk there to get an interview. I hid my dog in my pocket and jumped into the barbershop discussions like I fit in. I was there with another guy who wanted the job and we were watching my new boss, Joe, cut hair. I started making coffee mainly for me and the clients, then I told the other guy he wasn't getting hired and should leave because the owner was related to me. I knew I shouldn't have lied, but I was desperate to get this job. I then told Joe I needed money for the bus and I would come back in the morning and start work tomorrow. I told my neighbour, who had gangrene on his legs, that I found a job and I was going to move soon. I was the happiest woman in the world.

Joe taught me how to barber since I was a hairdresser, and I went for my barber's license. I learned how to straight blade shave and brush cut police officers' hair. The guys shared so many secrets with me and I was sworn to keep them. Besides, they could arrest me if I told you. I was now working a good full-time job, with a new work family that seemed to love me, and had my little dog. I lived paycheque to paycheque before going out with my new friends to find a new place to rent. Finally, a job I wasn't going to get fired at.

One day, a good-looking Afghan guy named Jeff came into the barbershop and started bringing me gifts. It made me feel pretty special. I went from rags to riches, dining at the best restaurants and spending all my time with him. He wanted me to retire from the barbershop and the next thing I knew, we were living at a five-star hotel in Bombay, India. Jeff would go to meetings with his friends, and I would swim and take tours all around India with a bodyguard, keeping rupees in my pocket to hand out to the poor. In the evening, we would sit on our balcony overlooking the Indian Ocean, going through magazines. Jeff would pick out designer outfits for me, then the next day, off I went to the seamstress to make my new wardrobe. I thought it made me look like those women in fancy magazines.

Jeff and I would travel back and forth from India to Canada and I would visit my mom and our dog. We did this for almost 10 years, but, like all good things, our wealth started to crumble. I started asking questions and wondering who these friends of Jeff's were. I realized I was in over my head and I needed to go back to my normal life, if that was possible.

Jeff sensed that I wanted to leave. He took my passport and would punish me and my dog if we were disobedient or wanted to leave. I was brainwashed into thinking he was the only person who loved me. I tried to leave and hid my dog and car with my mom, but she called and told me she found a note in the car requesting I go back to Jeff. How did he find out? I was scared, but I went back since I was running out of money and I couldn't go back to the barbershop after all my wealthy travels.

We moved back to Toronto, got a nice place, and I was able to take my mom on a Caribbean cruise. I convinced her how wonderful my life was with Jeff. But just when I felt safe, Jeff started to have financial difficulties and required me to service him every day at noon to ease his stress. I confided in a girlfriend and she thought that maybe I was involved in something over my head and that I needed to escape. I felt so scared, alone, and anxious. Every day when the clock hit noon, I would try to hide, find something to do or try to leave, but Jeff was adamant that my job was to serve him and if I didn't, I would be punished. I learned quickly that the service job was better than the punishment. Eventually, Jeff ended up going to jail, thank goodness, which was my ticket to a new life.

I started seeing a therapist and met some new friends who encouraged me to go back to finish high school. Rebuilding my life was hard. I went on welfare, was using the food bank, and living in a halfway home. It felt degrading, considering where I had just come from, and I cried a lot.

151

During this time, my adopted sister, Melanie, came to stay with me. She glorified my previous life with Jeff and our travels all over the world. I told her it was scary and I only wanted a normal life now by going back to school and supporting myself, rather than relying on a man. She was adamant about finding Jeff's friends in Vancouver and called me to tell me she found one and put me on the phone with him. I said I didn't want any trouble since I was starting a new life without Jeff. I was so angry she put me in this predicament. I told her to find new friends. A couple of months later, my sister went missing and to this day it's considered a cold case file. I have no idea how she disappeared off the face of the Earth. I don't know if she's alive or dead; though the detectives call me every once in a while, there have been no updates.

My therapist was very helpful and she encouraged me to do high school during the summer so that I could start college in September. When my grades were below average, the counsellor thought I needed a special class as it was suspected that I might have attention deficit disorder. To comprehend the classes, I needed to purchase hand-held recorders so I could replay the class at home at night slowly and be able to go back over what the teachers were talking about. I also decided to go to the math and English labs for free help in the evenings. I had a couple of teachers that were in shock when I brought my grades up from failing to A's. One even accused me of cheating, but I proved myself when I finished a three-year program in college with awards, the highest grade-point average, and most contributions to the school. I decided to keep going onward to university and received my bachelor's in Marketing, with a minor in Law.

My first job was as a bingo bunny for an online gaming company in a downtown Toronto loft. I would come up with ideas and work with a programmer to develop my thoughts, as well as talk to bingo players through an online chat. I was enjoying my job until the panic attacks started. I would be at my desk and then suddenly have to go to the washroom to have a panic attack.

My boss thought I was up to something fishy, having my friends visit and taking breaks, so he fired me. Little did he know I was getting support for my anxiety and dealing with extreme attacks that would paralyze me, leaving me out of breath and unable to concentrate.

My therapist at the time was teaching me cognitive therapy without drugs, which was so surreal and scary in itself. I had to write in a journal and open up very truthfully. I ended up confronting people from my past, which caused an uproar with my family but ended in healing and better relationships. I must say it was rocky for a while. After years of resenting my mom, I was now understanding her and we started over again. I would visit her and we grew quite close.

Sending out resumes and trying to find work was a full-time job in itself. I learned not to send out generic resumes as they were thrown out because companies wanted targeted resumes. This took more time but increased my chances at a job. I made a new best friend, Chris, and she helped me target my resume for each job I wanted. She took me out and showed me I could have an office like her and get that dream job. She was right! Hard work and dedication paid off. I began working at a college east of Toronto during the day and going to the same college at night for free to learn the courses I would teach during the day. I kind of felt like a phony because I was simply teaching these daytime students the courses I was learning at night, but the students said I made the class fun and they had no idea of the situation. This job caused me to be anxious and sometimes I felt like I was drowning. I knew I was in over my head, so I asked Chris to help me find another job before things got worse.

Chris also set me up with Ron, a tall, good-looking guy who would become my forever love. Ron and I moved in together and I got a new job in Ajax. Life was good again. I had a package, including dental and medical, and triple the salary with this new job as a Marketing & Customer Service Manager. It was mostly fun, except the staff were set in their ways and didn't appreciate my fresh ideas. I had many battles at work, and a lot more anxiety attacks, on my way to healing. I had to leave Ron in Mississauga during the week with his son, and rent a room in Ajax to focus on my new job and give it my full attention if I was to succeed. Ron and I only saw each other on weekends and missed each other so much.

Eventually, Ron and I purchased our first new home in Pickering that had a pool and big backyard. Ron's son came to live with us and our new life was amazing. Just as things were going well, I received word that my dad had died in Calgary. My crazy alcoholic dad had decided to take his own life and I felt so much guilt. The last time we had spoken, I got him off the phone quickly and told him I couldn't talk because I had my job to focus on. Dad had been drunk and wanted me to talk to his dog.

I found myself in therapy again, this time to deal with the guilt of not being the support my dad needed. The funeral home offered me free group counselling every week and I went with my journal to work through my emotions and guilt. The group taught me to accept my feelings and honour my process of healing in a group setting. There is no judgement in these groups and I highly recommend searching for one in your area if you have suffered a loss. I went through the denial, anger, bargaining, depression, and acceptance before coming out the other side, without the use of drugs, just writing and discussing my feelings.

The group counselling helped with my grief, but I still had this ugly invisible ailment called anxiety to deal with. When I was experiencing a lot of anxiety at work, I would stay late after everyone went home and focus in a quiet spot. During the day I would float around all bubbly, making my job look easy while I suffered in silence. When the company started to expand and new people came on board, my anxiety went through the roof. I was let go from my job after three years.

I was so devastated and in shock that I sunk into a dark place for weeks. Unsure of how we could pay our mortgage, we had to sell our home and move into an apartment building in Ajax. Ron blamed me for taking away his high life and I blamed myself for not being good enough. I told myself that I wasn't meant to have a big job with lots of money. When I was negative it seemed like things got worse. I fell in the grocery store and hurt myself. My neighbour at the time gave me painkillers and I found myself heading down a path of self-pity. I was so devastated and it took me months to recover, but I came through the other side and decided it was time to change my career. I didn't want to work with those big corporate people in a fancy office. I wanted to be happy.

I was tired of working for other people and always getting fired. I decided to start my own business and include Ron so we could always be together and he could quit his trucking job. I had a dream that I had a cleaning company named *Maid Mart*, so the next day I researched it and found the name was not taken. I decided to trademark the name, develop a logo, and start a website. The only problem was I didn't know how to clean, so I worked during the day for a local cleaner and at night for a janitorial company. Both companies took advantage of me and paid me very little money. Although I felt discouraged, I pressed forward. After months of going nowhere, I decided it was time to do it on my own. I was now ready to start my own business.

Living in Ajax on the 12th floor of an apartment building was not easy to start a cleaning company. I would take shopping carts of cleaning products down the elevator every day, which held up other tenants. All Ron wanted to do was sleep during the day in quiet and work at his nighttime job, while I was trying to build a life for us. I felt like he was drifting further away from me. He was always angry with me and I started finding pictures of another woman on his phone. I felt like I was becoming like my mother when I was a child, accusing Ron of infidelities the way my mom used to with my dad. The more I tried to get closer to him, the more he pulled away from me. Even though panic and fear set in, I kept going and hoped everything would get better.

I hired a local accountant to help me in the office so I could spend more time with Ron and my business. She ended up stealing my client while I was paying her to work for me. I couldn't believe that someone I trusted with my business would betray me. I had to start over and try to rebuild my tiny business. I learned to not feel sorry for myself because I was too busy trying to hold it together and keep what employees and clients I had left. I refused to give up even though we were going broke.

One day, a weekly client called and asked me why I was taking her dog out of the cage (she was watching me on her cameras). I stated the dog needed to learn to walk and she harshly advised me not to do that again. Being the animal lover I was, I continued to take the dog from her cage and teach her to walk and play while my staff cleaned her home every week. She called me again to say she was putting the dog down and it was my fault for letting the dog out of the cage. My mind went back to my stray dog, Buddy, I had as a child, and how my mom put him in an animal shelter when I was a teenager. I suddenly felt a deep loss and pain beyond words. I called her back and begged her to let me find a home for the dog. She said if I was there before her husband came home, I could have the dog, otherwise, it was going to the pound. I drove so fast and frantic to her house and ran past her husband to the dog that was thrown into my arms. I named the dog Dusty "the cleaning dog" and I now had a new partner in grime to travel around with.

Dusty was now the *Maid Mart* mascot and I took her everywhere. I had a fur-baby to love, who gave me unconditional love in return, and nobody would ever take that away from me again. We went to construction clean-ups, residential homes, senior homes, carpet jobs, reno jobs, and Dusty never left my side.

Many clients started requesting Dusty come to cleaning jobs, including Francis, a 92-year-old client I had. Dusty would sit with Francis in her wheelchair while we cleaned. One night, her husband called me to say Francis was dying in the hospital and her last request was to see Dusty. So, we snuck into the hospital with Dusty in a bag to see Francis, and her husband attributed this to her living an additional two years after that.

Ron and I started to hit a rough patch in our relationship. I would watch TV alone at night after work with Dusty and eat a lot. The more weight I gained, the more Ron worked later and later and was never home. I felt isolated, alone, and depressed at feeling him drift away. Then, one of the cleaners invited me to go dancing with the girls. It was hard to fix myself up and get the energy to go out and have fun because I only wanted to wallow in my emotional pain. But when I forced my chubby body out to go dancing, I felt better. I started to feel pretty when I dressed up and started caring about myself. So, I began to go every Thursday night dancing with the girls, and with this newfound love for myself, I found the confidence to start confronting Ron on his behaviour. Unfortunately, it only caused more fighting and distance between us.

To save our relationship, Ron and I decided to buy a smaller, fixer-upper home in Oshawa, and we ran my cleaning business and his renovation company out of the house. Despite this, he still could not let go of his full-time trucking job, which was exhausting him. Half of the house I used for *Maid Mart* and the other half was home with Ron and Dusty. I worked hard to try to keep it all together, and just when I thought life was getting better, I found more pictures of a woman on Ron's phone. The fear and anxiety started back again and I would have really bad anxiety attacks. Ron was never home and I was always working, which made me feel so alone and scared. I asked my mom to come to visit to help me figure things out and she promised me she would eventually find out if Ron was having an affair.

After a while, life in Oshawa was back to normal and business was booming. Ron was getting reno jobs and seemed happier. Then, I got a call that would change my life forever – my mom had died while in Guatemala helping the needy. My mom was the one person who promised to solve my mysteries and listen to all my fears. A couple of weeks after her death, while standing in the kitchen, I screamed at her and God: "You promised to find out if Ron was cheating, and now you're gone!" All of a sudden, I had this voice telling me to go get some of those hand-held recorders I bought in college and place them around the cars and house to find out if Ron is cheating.

I became obsessed with working during the day and listening to the recordings of Ron's shenanigans during the night after he had fallen asleep. I would call my brother, as well as my friend,

Cheri, to share my findings with them. Dusty and I were on the couch every night grieving the loss of my mom and trying to find evidence on Ron. One day, the inevitable happened and I heard evidence of Ron and one of my employees in our bedroom making love. I had a hard choice to make: I could either walk away from our 18-year relationship or I could forgive Ron and stay.

I decided to take Ron and his kids out for Valentine's Day at his favourite restaurant. I would look into Ron's eyes and let him know how much I truly loved him. If he reciprocated the love, I would stay, but if he didn't then I would end it. When the moment came, I told Ron how much I loved him and that I wanted to make things work. He looked down in shame and I knew it was over.

We came back home and I fell asleep on the couch with Dusty, again making my excuse that I was still in deep grief over the loss of my mom. A couple of hours later, Ron came out of the bedroom, demanding I come to bed now and that it was my duty to be his wife and look after his needs.

This took me back to my mom's stories of her having to stay with my dad after his affairs because she married him and it was against the church to leave him. I decided at that moment not to be like my mom. I proceeded to take Dusty to the basement where the kids were and told them I was about to confront their father about his affair. They sat there in shock. Our lives were about to change forever.

I spent the next couple of hours confronting Ron, while he denied ever cheating on me in 18 years. But I had proof and I told myself to stay strong. I felt so anxious about possibly losing this man I loved so much, but I couldn't allow myself to be with a cheater. Someone was going to have to leave and it was going to be me and Dusty.

I called the girls from work and my brother, and they helped me put all my stuff in storage. I left the house to Ron and the kids and off I went to live in the side of the garage with my dog. There I was starting over again. It was one of the loneliest and hardest times of my life. I cried a lot and would watch the house through my garage window, while Ron walked many girlfriends through our home and the kids continued with their lives. I felt like I never existed and had wasted a great deal of my time. I used this time to be alone and figure things out. I put all my focus on my business, my employees, and my clients.

I was reaching a point of feeling a little stronger when Ron came knocking on my door. He told me he was going to kill himself if I didn't take him back. I did not want his blood on my hands or his kids not forgiving me, so we agreed to be friends. We began a journey of healing together and talked about what we could have done differently in the past. We both learned a new respect for each other and both figured out we could stay best friends and started sharing all our fears, hopes, and dreams with each other. We grew closer than the last few years we'd been together, and people thought it was strange to be best friends with my ex.

We even started working together on projects just like I had wanted when I opened my company, and he finally quit his trucking job. I still loved him so deeply but I just had to hide my love and act strong because he loved so many women and had a hard time staying true.

I decided it was time for me to go out and have some fun of my own, so I went to a party and brought Dusty with me. Everyone at the party loved Dusty and she had so much fun getting lots of attention and people to play with her. On the way home, Dusty started vomiting all over the car, so I pulled over but she couldn't stop. I was so scared and wondering what was happening to my baby? I turned around and took her to an animal clinic and they asked me what she ate. I called the girls from the party and they said Dusty loved the pork so much they just kept feeding it to her. The vet told me pig meat is fatty and deadly for dogs and Dusty would have to stay in the hospital for weeks if she was to live. It would cost me thousands of dollars, that I didn't have, and I was told if I didn't have the money, I should put her down.

I stayed for the rest of the day at the clinic in the waiting room, crying and asking God to let Dusty live. The clinic was closing and the vet said I could save money if I took Dusty home at night hooked up to an intravenous because they would just be keeping her in a kennel all night. I took her home and kept her warm in my arms at night and then had to part with her during the day to go to work while she was in the clinic.

After a week, the vet called me and said she had something to tell me and asked me to come into the clinic because she didn't want to tell me while I was driving. The *Maid Mart* girls and I cried and drove so fast to the clinic before I pushed through reception and dropped at Dusty's cage. I was worried I was going to hear the worst, but the news was that Dusty was fine and was ready to go home – Thank you, God!

I moved from my little apartment back into the house alone. Ron asked me to take back the house because he was unable to look after it and he wanted to be as free as a bird. I felt free too. With this new freedom I started dancing, dating, and enjoying my life again, but if I wanted to be truly free, I needed to buy Ron out and own the house myself. I started praying and went to see a lawyer. Ron became resentful and wouldn't sign anything. He wanted me to pay the bills, look after the house, and have the security of a home to come back to if none of his women friends worked out. So, I settled into this agreement, took care of the home and Ron helped out when he could.

Although, with Ron not living there I needed more help around the house now.

One night while listening to Steve Harvey on YouTube, he was saying how God saved him from many trials and tribulations and how he follows a couple of Bible verses. One verse he mentioned was from Habakkuk 2:2. King James Version: "And the Lord answered me, and said, Write the vision, and make it plain upon tables, that he may run that readeth it." So, I went to the dollar store and purchased three large pieces of cardboard with sticky notes and coloured pencils. On one board I wrote 'Ask,' on the second board I wrote 'Claim,' and on the third board I wrote 'Maid Mart.' I put each one behind my desk in the office and left sticky notes there to do postings. These were my boards to ask God to answer my prayers and to track which ones were getting answered. The first on my 'Ask' board was to be able to buy Ron out and be mortgage-free. A couple of years later, Ron asked me to buy him out as long as he could still have free access to the garage for life. We made a deal and I moved the request to buy Ron out from the 'Ask' board to the 'Claim' board. The process was working. Thanks, Steve Harvey!

As I continued my journey to rebuilding my life, I ended up with a dog named Ginger who had been injured after being thrown down the stairs in a cage. I took Ginger to the vet and had her stitched up, then started looking for a home for her.

The vet said I must disclose to possible adopters that Ginger was probably going to have brain damage. It was hard to find someone to take her, so I ended up keeping Ginger. The girls at *Maid Mart* wondered how I would manage two dogs and a business on my own and said I should give her to the shelter. I didn't want to let that happen. She was part of the family now, and, like Dusty, I also brought Ginger with me on the job. She learned quickly from Dusty as we did jobs at big sites and empty homes.

I still asked God to give me the right staff. On my 'Ask' board I wrote: "Please bring me a dependable employee." One Friday, I had two cleaners who were constantly undermining me and decided not to show up for work and making lame excuses. I went outside to cry and wondered how I would clean three houses alone. Cindy, a woman who had been filling in and was cleaning the deck, looked at me and said, "It's okay, I'll go with you and we can clean the houses together." She was a woman of God and I felt like my mom had sent her to help me. My prayers were answered and Cindy is still a loyal and appreciated employee at *Maid Mart*.

When my mom died, I received her journals, so I decided to start reading them every night. I learned how she had handled being a single mom. I learned that she was very poor and that she had a friend, Reha, who would help us by bringing us food and giving our family money. She was my mom's best friend. My mom went off welfare and got a job as a secretary at the church. She started caring more for others than she did herself, even though she could hardly afford to feed us. I learned that I was a selfish teenager and I could have done more to contribute. As I read all of these journal entries she wrote, I would cry and write in my journal. Why didn't I try more to understand her back then? But reading my mom's journals helped me understand something now. Instead of focusing on my circumstances, I needed to focus on others, so from that day forward, I started giving back and letting God look after the rest.

Writing in my journal made me realize that crying and feeling sorry for myself was an attitude I needed to change. Now was the time to start putting my employees first above my own needs and giving back to society. I started randomly going out and giving things to people on the street. I found when I started putting things on my 'Ask' board, little miracles were granted.

I was still dealing with my anxiety, though, and I wondered how I would handle all the bills and mortgage alone. I was listening to fear instead of living in faith. In the service industry, you never know when you can lose a client, and sometimes that was scary. One day, I got a call that I was going to lose my biggest client with five offices at the end of the month. I began to wonder if I attracted this situation by allowing fear into my life. I knew better than to feed fear since it just attracts more. I started praying and researching meditation classes and found a local spirit group close by in a community centre. I started attending Wednesday night meditation classes and Sunday church with lunch included. Every Sunday morning, I was ready to go to the front and ask for prayer. It seemed right after receiving a healing prayer, I would be able to get through a week without panic attacks. I was the only one going up every week, but it helped me, so I started going first just to make sure I received a healing prayer.

At work, I started filling out my schedule and noticed at times I did not have clients to clean for. How could I find work for my employees? Just as I did with my dream boards, I put requests to God on the calendar and like magic every week the blank spots would get filled. I was grateful to be able to provide for my employees so they could feed their families.

Things turned around for the worse when one of my long-time trusted employees went behind my back and decided she would start her own cleaning business. She told all the clients how dumb I was and that she would be a better choice. She went after my top clients and left us with the smaller ones. Soon, clients started calling and telling me I was a horrible manager because this employee was taking over and they were firing me. Then, the government called me and said I owed this

164

employee compensation for years of work and that I owed her thousands of dollars, which I didn't have. In a moment of despair, I put on my 'Ask' board, "How the heck are you going to get me out of this one?"

I called my brother and asked him for advice. He told me to not hold any resentment, forgive her, and move forward by going out there to get more clients. How could I forgive someone who stole my clients and told them lies about me to steal the business that I'd worked so hard for? It wasn't easy, and the anxiety, panic, and fear reared their ugly head, but I chose to push forward. Cindy came to me and said the girls are asking how will *Maid Mart* survive this employee who took all our good clients? I told her to keep the faith and tell the employees it would be okay. I believed that God would look after us.

I had a friend, Joe, at a local newspaper who decided to help me fight the government on giving this former employee money. I also had another owner of a cleaning company in Ajax help me. With both of their help, I rebuilt from the ground up, kicking, crying, and screaming all the way. Despite my hard work to rebuild my business, the government decided to shut me down for default on not paying my HST. All bank accounts were closed and a demand letter came stating I owed a lot of money. It was Friday, the girls were coming for their pay, and I had nothing, so I called my brother and told him what happened. He came with thousands of dollars just as my employees arrived and we paid them all with cash. My brother saved my reputation and my life at that moment.

Again, I had to refinance to get the money to pay back the government, as well as my brother. I started cleaning offices at night and working with the girls to rebuild the business. When I decided to trust God and have faith, I received a call the big client with the five offices was back and missed *Maid Mart*! Soon, other bigger clients came when they heard about *Maid*

Mart through word of mouth. I focused on paying my employees so they could feed their families, as well as being able to feed my dogs, which meant that sometimes I could not afford food for myself.

I received news from the government that I didn't have to pay any compensation to my former employee who stole my company clients. She still had the clients and would spread lies about me, but I just prayed for her and turned it over to God, and went on. I wrote in my journal and forgave her. I found forgiveness is the only real way to move forward, plus I didn't have time to feed the evil in it all. I am blessed and I guess it goes back to my gramma always praying for me my entire life. I took a lot of wrong turns in life but now I was trying to stay on the right path. As clients started coming back, new ones also came on board. We even won an award for the most voted cleaning company in Durham Region. *Maid Mart* was growing and life was looking good.

One day, a long-time client called me and asked if I could watch their dog, Chico, while they went on vacation because their dog sitter bailed on them. I said yes, figuring it was fine to have an extra dog around for one week, but I didn't consider the fact that Ginger was not fixed and neither was Chico. The outcome was four little puppies, one born deformed and almost didn't make it. I kept the deformed puppy and called him Pee Wee. He was tiny and didn't promise to live very long, but he ended up growing to be the biggest of all of Ginger's puppies and is still part of the family. Pee Wee is the most adorable, loving dog who loves kids and the *Maid Mart* girls. Now I was a single woman with three dogs, 10 fish, one bird, and lots of employees to look after. God was looking after the bills and I was working long, hard hours. I went back to my 'Ask' board and requested fewer working hours, a new smart accountant, and loyal employees and friends.

Everything seemed like it was picking up and life was good again. I was attending church, listening to YouTube in the morning, writing in my journal, and becoming a stronger, better woman. I had a great relationship with Ron and I was able to find him lots of renovations jobs.

On January 10th, 2021 at 6 a.m. I received a life-changing phone call. There's something about people calling me early in the morning that usually represents sad news. It was Ron's son and he was crying hysterically, saying that Ron was in a tragic car accident. How could this be? He had just been at my house the night before. I was in disbelief. The love of my life was gone with no hope to ever reunite. All I could do was write this poem through my tears:

Little Crispy Snowflakes – by Beverley Rose Lynn Thomson, for Ron Miller

Little crispy snowflakes falling on my face…
I feel your breath in the wind whisk by.
The wind forces my face to crispy snow tracks.
Tracks so fresh from yesterday's visit.
The gates of heaven have opened.
You've been called to see your maker.
The snow will melt; the tracks will fade.
I'm left with your breath and little snowflakes.
I look out the window and await your arrival.
To no avail, you're really gone (heartbreaking).

A horn "beeps" …a white car drove by!
I jump to see… is it you? Or, is it just crispy snowflakes?

The hands on the clock say go to bed.
My hands say no, go outside and feel the crispy tracks.

I touch the snow, feel the last memory.
The only thing left… is crispy little snowflakes.

With Ron gone, I felt like I was really on my own with the house, the business, the employees, and life's challenges. Time has changed me, I'm stronger, I've walked through grief without prescriptions to numb the feelings. It's amazing to look back on my journals and realize how far I've come. Today, if you give me a problem, I'll give you a solution. Life is too short to waste another moment trapped in a pity party of fear. I choose to live my life not being negative and feeling sorry for myself, but rather to share myself openly in the hopes that it helps others from wasting another precious moment. I realize now that my thoughts created my emotions, which triggered my feelings of anxiety and panic. I am the only one with the power to change my life, so I choose every day to change my thoughts before they take me hostage with panic and destruction. I no longer live with fear and truly feel free. Words, relationships, death, and challenges can't knock me down anymore.

As I reflect on how I got to where I am today, I am proud of how I carved my own spiritual path. I listen to motivational speakers on social media every morning, and at night I shut off the TV and fall asleep listening to meditations on how to manifest wealth and spiritual healing into my life. I talk to my angel guides and Jesus, read books, and sometimes attended church. I never put myself down and I always ask God for what I want and need. I never forget to thank God for all miracles and I'm constantly reminded of them when I look at my 'Ask' and 'Claim' boards in my office.

Today, I walk in faith with my three fur babies. We live a simple life, go to the beach for walks, eat good healthy food, and spend time with staff and friends. I have the best accountant in the world who helps me organize my emails and pays my taxes every month on time. I have faithful employees that have been with *Maid Mart* for years, and we work as a team for our clients. I feel completely free, naturally high, and grateful every day for my new life without fear or anxiety.

I am here to tell others who've experienced anxiety that there is hope. I thank all those who have supported me along the way; relatives, friends, and my brother, Tim, for always encouraging me to be a better person.

I couldn't have done it without all of you! People think I'm naturally high, but I tell them I'm free!

Dedication

This story is dedicated to the unknown Filipino woman that donated her time free of charge to tutor me in math and English when I was in college. And next

To my long-lost friend, Sheryl, whom I recently reconnected with, and who pushed me to get up and keep going during my saddest point in my life.

To Chris, who took me under her wing for years, nourished me with love, and encouraged me to go back to school and accomplish what I would have thought was impossible.

To Cheri, who held my hand when my mom died and my relationship fell apart.

To Laura, who always encourages me to look after my health and enjoy nature.

Also, to one of my old bosses for teaching me how *not* to treat my present-day employees.

But most of all, to Tim Thomson, my best friend and brother, who taught me that when you procrastinate you feel like you're drowning, so now every year, we make a bet to see who will win the procrastination battle as a way to stay motivated. Tim, I truly love you, I thank you for your life-long support. Oh, and yes, you lost the bet baby!

Me & Timmy Dad's Driving School I was 5 years old

Me and my Dad

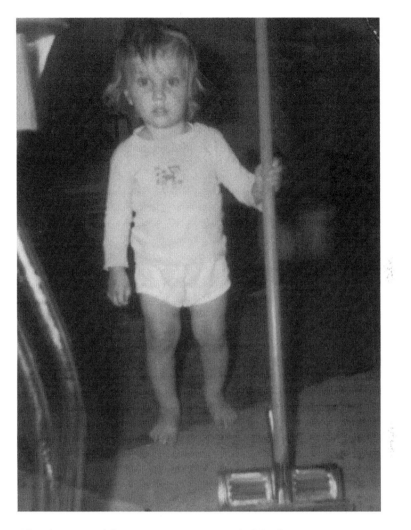

Cleaning started from young I was awarded for it

Christmas with Santa Timmy and I

Me and Dad in California

In India

Christmas 2021

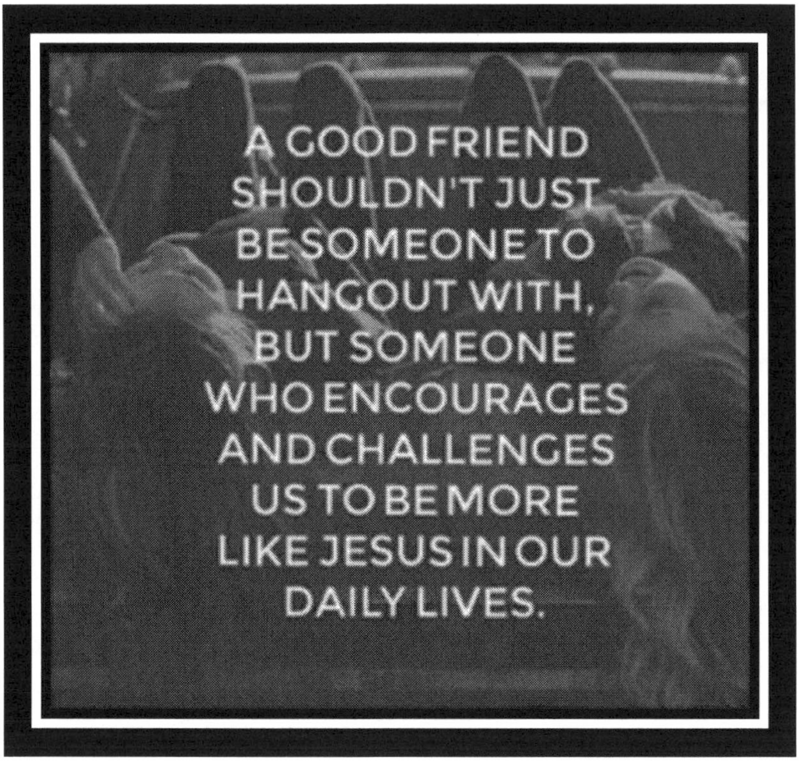

A GOOD FRIEND
SHOULDN'T JUST
BE SOMEONE TO
HANGOUT WITH,
BUT SOMEONE
WHO ENCOURAGES
AND CHALLENGES
US TO BE MORE
LIKE JESUS IN OUR
DAILY LIVES.

Mackenzie's World!

By Mackenzie Lubeck

Ever since I was five years old, I dreamed of being a model, and when I was 16, I made that dream a reality. It was difficult to do it, though, when I was younger, because my family didn't know exactly where to go for me to get modelling jobs. As a child, I was involved in dance for 10 years, did some gymnastics, and stage musicals for five years. As I got older, I started watching fashion runway shows and it made me want to pursue my dreams even more. Seeing those beautiful, tall women show their confidence pushed my dreams forward and I knew I wanted to do this. It was very inspiring for me, and now I've been a model for four years.

Deciding to pursue modelling meant that I would have to concentrate on it fully and put my other interests on hold. Going into modelling was exciting and I was ready to give it my all. My Nana is my 'NANAGER.' She runs my account for me and helps me get jobs in the industry, which is good. I wish I was more of an influencer though. Growing up, I always wanted to do a YouTube channel, but I just never knew how to do it because recording myself got confusing and editing seemed impossible.

Besides my model account, which is more of my portfolio, I have my Snapchat and my personal page where I post photos that are more of the real me and my daily life. I'm signed with two agencies, one in Florida and one in Toronto, though I mostly enjoy freelancing. I get most of my jobs myself, so everyone I know in this industry is from getting out there and making connections. Finding a way to get big brands to connect with is very difficult because they all want agency girls who are very tall, or who are with big agencies, all of which, of course, only accept models who are 5'9" and up. I believe height doesn't always bring talent and they should be more open to models of all sizes.

I've learned that you don't need to be the perfect, tall blonde with blue eyes and long legs. I'm 5'4", my hair color is always changing and my eyes are brown. I believe my personality is the thing that lights up and gets me noticed. Being a model is more about confidence and not so much about beauty anymore, in my opinion. It's about being you, flaws and all.

It hasn't always been easy for me to find confidence, though. I dealt with a lot of bullying when I was in elementary school. You'd think girls would be sweet and kind, but that certainly wasn't the case for me. I was bullied through grades three to seven, and my bullies were close friends and people I trusted. It all started through an online app and on Facebook. A girl who I thought was one of my best friends told me that there was a fake account made about me. It turned out that it was her behind the whole thing. She just wanted me to see it so that I would be upset and it would tear me down. It was hard to accept the fact that the person who I thought was my best friend for so many years just wanted to hurt me and ruin my life, all because I was doing what I love. The thing about bullying is that you never know when it could happen and who could end up doing those things to you. I finally switched schools in grade eight and it was the best decision for me at that time. I made so many friends and finally felt that I belonged for who I was.

In elementary school, I was not a popular kid and did not have the look that people wanted. I was very skinny and wore glasses. I had my small group of friends and that was enough for me. However, I did things that I guess made other kids jealous. I wasn't trying to rub anything in anyone's face, but I would invite friends over and give them things. It's just who I am. If someone wants or needs something I want to give it to them or do my best to get it for them to make them happy, even it's something of mine that I don't need as much as them. I've always loved helping and supporting people.

Going to high school was a fresh start. I had my friends from dance, but lost all of my elementary school friends and had nobody left that I'd grown up with. Although this made me sad, life in high school showed me that mean girls never change and will leave others behind just to move on to someone else. I've moved on though. I may not be the most confident person but I have enough confidence to get me by in life and I use it also to help lift others. I try to be happy and brave, and no longer hide myself. On the days where I might feel stuck and cry myself to sleep, I wake up and remind myself that it was just a bad moment, that I can move on, and that I will be okay.

One thing I would say about bullying is to not let it get the best of you. Always believe that you are amazing and strong, and never be afraid to stand up for yourself when someone has done you wrong. I found the best way to try to deal with bullying was to have a good support system and remember that you are worthy of great things and a happy life. We don't have to be the victim and our bullies don't define who we truly are. We don't have to feel bad for wanting a wonderful life. I realized the problem was the bullies and not anything I had done. We don't know the hardships people go through behind closed doors. Their life may be difficult, so they take it out on others to try to make themselves feel better and to maybe not feel so alone. As the victim, you may focus on how the bullying makes you feel. I believe we should also think about what our bully is going through. It didn't just happen on its own. Someone or something has taught them to be this way. This is why I choose to be the strong person in the situation; to not only be confident in who I am and what I love about myself, but to also not turn around and treat bullies the way they've treated me or to break them down more than they already are.

My experience with bullying is happening less and less, but I still struggle every day from what happened to me. I am not the same person I was 10 years ago. I'm so different now and more confident in myself. I am happy and believe in myself, but I still have days when I feel completely and utterly awful about myself because I will be reminded of the people who tried to make me feel bad about who I am. In those tough moments, I almost start to believe it's true until I stop myself and remember that I will be okay, that I can get through this, and that I will persevere one way or another. I believe that you should never give up on yourself and remember that you are perfect the way you are. Be true to yourself and never try to be someone else, because if you do, you won't fit into your proper placement in life. You will instead feel like you're stuck or drowning in the deepest of water and unable to breathe.

For the most part, I just try to stay focused. It's not always easy to do. Some days are harder than others, and some days words can hurt. I just remind myself that this is my journey and my life, and not that of my bullies. Remembering to spread kindness as much as possible is one thing that helps me get through it.

I have taken the lessons I've learned and have used that to help me through the many struggles I have encountered along the way. For example, I got to a point with one photographer that made me feel like he wanted to keep me to himself and showed signs of being possessive. I think he realized I was serious about wanting to be a model and it became a bit of an obsession with him. He saw me as this girl who would make him famous and he took my talent into his own hands. I felt like I was being held back and started to have some doubts of really wanting to pursue modelling, as well as wondering if I was even right for this industry. But I showed him that I'm strong and confident in myself. I've learned from my past and know not to let someone take advantage of me. After giving it a lot of thought, and taking a little break, I realized that this was still my passion, and it was best to leave that controlling person behind. I discovered that I deserve my dreams and my journey is not for anyone else but me. We all deserve this!

After this experience, I started reaching out to other photographers and brands on my own and started to get paid work. I tried not to get discouraged, kept working hard, and remained confident as I moved forward.

Now, at 19 years old, I can say that life is truly an amazing journey. There have been closed doors, open doors, and doors you wish you didn't go through, but the ones that make your heart burst are the ones that are worth opening. In this industry, it's all about what's next and to keep going. Sometimes it's hard to keep pushing forward, especially when it feels the whole world goes against you. In some ways, it's like the Covid-19 pandemic. Before the pandemic, I had so many cool opportunities that I could tell you about, but honestly, I wasn't ready to go on any of them. I think it's because I didn't feel I was prepared to just leave my home and family.

One thing the pandemic has proven is that I am ready to move ahead and take advantage of all the opportunities that come my way now, and I can't wait for the modelling industry to return to normal.

My journey as a model has been great overall. I've been in *New York Fashion Week*, as well as many other fashion shows. I'm looking forward to more big runways in the future, as I've done some in my home area and they were fun. I come alive on the runway! I remember in NYFW when another model told me to calm down from dancing. I was so happy to finally be hitting that runway, so I got on there and lit that stage up for every girl who felt like they weren't enough to be there. I believe that every girl was meant to be there and anyone can have their superstar moment!

My advice to everyone is to just never give up on what you want in life, no matter what. We all have value and we all deserve to see the world exactly how we grew up wanting to see it. Don't let your younger self disappear completely as you grow up. Make yourself proud by achieving everything you've ever wanted to. I'm excited to get out there, make a name for myself, and become who I've always dreamed of being. Money can't buy all happiness but doing what you love can!

Dedication

This is dedicated to all those that have believed in me and supported my dreams this far. Love you all. Never stop believing and reaching for the stars!

Photography Dale Mann wearing SQJ

Photo credit John Ceko

Photo credit littlebunniphotog

186

Photographer Michael Leahey

Photographer Paul Iacoviello

Photographer Terry Marshall

In Honour of a dear friend deceased 2021

189

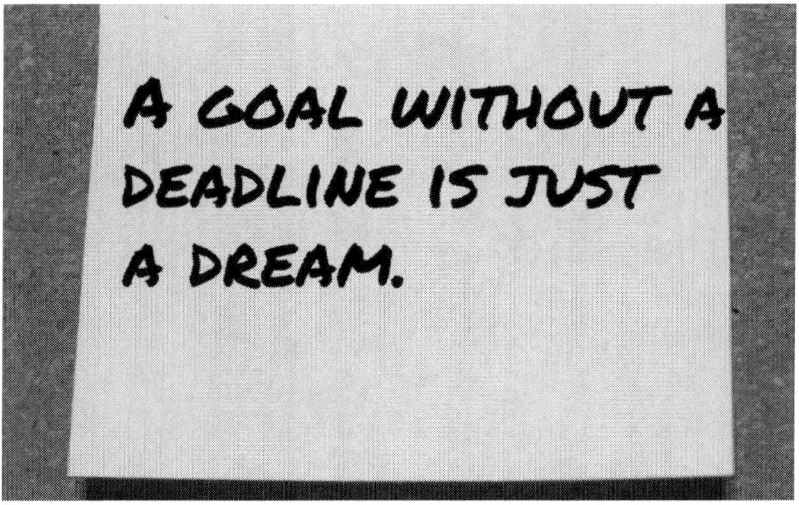
A GOAL WITHOUT A
DEADLINE IS JUST
A DREAM.

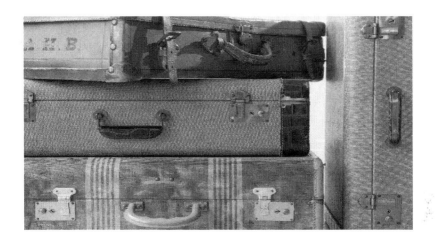

A Dream Come True: My Journey

By Sutha Shanmugarajah

"You'll see it when you believe it." ~ Wayne Dyer

Back Home and Back to the Past

I was born in a country where a girl's beauty is defined by her skin tone. The lighter your complexion is, the more beautiful you were perceived.

During my childhood, I recall family members and neighbours making remarks such as, "So and so had a baby girl and she looks dark," or "Did you know, Raja's wife had a baby girl and she looks fair?" This kind of talk is still vivid in my mind today and is still very disturbing. Why is there so much emphasis on skin tone?

To some parents, skin tone was a concern as it presented a financial burden. It would be more difficult to find a suitor for a daughter with a darker complexion than a lighter one. In such cases, parents would have to secure a larger dowry to marry off a daughter with a darker skin tone. This would have a huge impact on families who were already struggling financially.

Sad, but true.

This affected the girls and not the boys of the family. It was an undermining way of defining beauty based on your skin tone and discrimination in many ways. As I was growing up, I was placed in the dark skin category. They called me 'black.' My sister and some of my cousins were lighter in skin tone and were classified as beautiful. I grew up believing they were better looking than me. It created a complexity among girls with darker skin, since this was the environment in which they were raised. Girls judged themselves on the colour of their skin. If they felt they were too dark, they would try to lighten their face by grinding turmeric root and applying it to their face to make it look fairer and brighter. Girls would select certain colours of clothing that would make their skin look fairer.

A New Home, A Different Life

At age nine, I immigrated to Canada and, unlike where I came from, I was surrounded by people of different backgrounds, cultures, ethnicity, colour, and race. As I started to mingle with different ethnic groups, I started to feel more comfortable in my own skin. But, when I spent time with members of my community, I felt very uncomfortable.

We immigrated to Canada because of Civil War in Sri Lanka. We hardly had much to start our new life in Canada and it was very difficult for many years. My parents' income was just sufficient enough to meet our daily needs. Beauty products, such as lipsticks, eyeliner, and eye shadows, seemed far out of my reach and unaffordable, but, even if they were available to me, I felt I was not worthy of having them.

I began to feel different when I started working as I gained self-confidence. I was able to overlook the judgement placed on my skin tone, which allowed me to feel more comfortable with members of my community. Interacting with people of other ethnic groups built my confidence even more. Compliments, such as, "Your skin tone is beautiful!" would take me by surprise. I found it strange and kind of funny when people would tell me they were looking forward to the hot weather so they can tan their skin, or when they were going to the tanning salon for the same reason. For them, darker skin spelled beauty. Very amusing! The women in my community, instead, look for products, like "FAIR & LOVELY" to make their skin fairer.

An Arranged Marriage

When I completed my studies in university, I wanted to get married and start a family. In some ways, I felt compelled to follow the traditions I grew up with, and, in my early 20s, I permitted my parents to look for someone they thought would be a good match for me. This arrangement would be based on the horoscopes of the two people. An astrological book is written when a baby is born; the time of birth, the day and month, as well as the year, are key elements in matching you to someone suitable.

There is a marriage broker, who will have a file of eligible single candidates' charts that were given by friends, family, or relatives who are looking for an ideal match for their son/daughter/friend. Once a marriage broker receives a request, they will go through their files and see if there are any matches. The marriage broker, with their knowledge of astrology, would recommend matches that would be successful.

Once the broker establishes a match, they are responsible for notifying both sides. Photos are then exchanged. If there is an attraction or interest to meet, the families would make the arrangement.

When this process got started, I was quite excited! I was looking forward to marrying someone nice and kind. The meeting place would be the temple, and this was arranged by my father. I had faith that the horoscope would bring a suitable match. To my disappointment, I later learned that the match was not solely based on the horoscope, but on the caste, family origins, education of the parents and groom, employment, how much assets the family had, and the list goes on. It seemed more like a business arrangement to me.

For my first arrangement, we arrived at the temple and met the other family. My parents engaged in a conversation with them, and I had no opportunity to talk to the guy. I was young and shy, and I followed my parents' advice. This is how most arranged marriages are like. My first experience was nerve-wracking. I came home and my father asked me what I thought about the guy. Without me responding, he said the guy and his family seem like good people. Should we proceed? I didn't know what to say. I was silent. My dad picked up the phone and called the marriage broker and replied "Yes." The moment you say "Yes," and also the other side says "Yes," they start arranging the engagement/marriage registration and celebration. I was so confused. I just went along with it. One week passed by and we didn't hear from the broker and my father was anguished. He kept on calling the broker. Two weeks later, we found out that this guy was interested in another girl he met at school and the parents knew about it, but his parents still wanted him to go for the arranged marriage. It upset me right away and I started to feel that this arranged marriage thing was not for me. But my father would not stop. He would continue to place photos of suitable guys on my desk and ask if I would be interested in meeting him and the family. Since I didn't want to hurt my family, I went ahead with these meetings. After a while, I started to get annoyed and frustrated. As time passed (this went on for over five years), my dad noticed I was making more excuses not to meet anyone. He was getting upset. He went to the extent of having the marriage broker speak to me. The broker would stress that I was getting old and it was time for me to get married. They would advise me on what dress/saree I should wear for the photos. They would advise me to wear makeup so I will look fair in the profile pictures that they share with the potential mate. There was always more pressure on the girl and her family. The pressure became too much, and I agreed to see another potential match after a long time. This time it was a little different. Both sides agreed for us to meet on our own. I started to talk about my ambitions and what I wanted to do in the future with my education. He didn't care much about my ambitions or dreams and he just went straight to talk about me taking care of him and his family. At that point, I'd had enough.

I went home and told my father that I can't do this anymore. We had arguments for many years, and I pulled away from all of this by focusing on what I truly wanted to do in my life. I walked away from relatives and friends who kept on nagging me about being single and bringing my mood down.

I walked away from all the traditional marriage talk, all the conversations I had with the brokers, meeting different families, and having arguments with my dad, which initially stressed me out and made me unhappy. Over time, I placed my focus on things I wanted to do, and, in doing so, I gained self-confidence and independence. The thought of getting married and starting a family was far from my mind.

I am happy with what I have done over the years, and I am happy that I helped so many people along the way. Sometimes people say that they feel sorry for me that I am not married and don't have children yet. But everyone has a purpose in life and that is what I am following. The whole arranged marriage was putting me in a position where I felt that I didn't have the freedom to live my life as I wanted. After all, I believe marriage should be based on love, not looks, money, status, religion, etc. I'm grateful for the time and energy my dad put into making this work. As a parent, he did his duty.

Communication

My interest and passion for serving society led me to gain public speaking skills. One day, when I was surfing the Internet, I came across a public speaking program. The program seemed interesting, but I didn't take any action at that time, apart from reading about it. A couple of years later, I became interested once again and started to look for more details regarding the time and places for these meetings. I attended one of the meetings but was not sure if I wanted to join. To my surprise, a year after that I got an e-mail at work informing me that a new public speaking club from that very same program was starting in the hospital where I was working, and that was when a bell rang in my head. There is a connection between this program and myself, and I decided to invest more time to learn about it. I attended one of the meetings and the rest is history! I was impressed with how those meetings were organized and how they were conducted.

At the end of every meeting, I was always happy, excited, and looking forward to the next one. Each meeting was full of excitement! The more meetings I attended, the more I learned from other members' speeches, evaluations, and impromptu sessions, and it helped me to improve myself. I was very enthusiastic about the program and agreed to take on one of the executive roles as Vice President of Public Relations. This role helped me a lot and gave me more opportunities to grow further. I was able to create the club website, worked on the club newsletter, and help in other activities to promote the club. After one year, I started to think outside the club and took on the Area Governor role, where I showed my self-confidence and leadership skills. This took me to another level, and I started to get acquainted with more members in District 60. There were many friendly and helpful members who wanted to help me achieve my goals. With their help, I grew as a leader during those years. I realized taking on the role as the Area Governor was the right decision as I developed valuable skills. While I was working as the Area Governor, I had the opportunity to learn from more advanced members of the public speaking program and went through training monthly. Not only did I end up getting selected as the Area Governor of the year, but I was also presented with the District 60 Area Governor Trophy! I am thankful for those great mentors and hardworking members who were dedicated to the program.

What's Next?

When I was the Area Governor, I found out that there was another role that was waiting for me. It was the Youth Leadership Program that was offered by the international division of the public speaking program. My interest in dealing with youth brought me to take on this role. This was one of the amazing opportunities that I've taken on and was very grateful to the organization for it. My mission for the program was to expose youth to public speaking so that they would develop the communication and leadership skills they needed to be successful in their future.

I am happy to say that this mission was a success! We had about nine youths who have completed the program and are happy that they took part in it. At their last class, each one of them had to present an inspirational/motivational speech. They did a great job! We asked them at the end of the session to tell us their opinion about the program, and the majority of them mentioned that they would recommend it to their friends. As much as we taught these kids, we also learned a lot from them! Learning is a journey, and this public speaking program is a great place to continue that journey! As for myself, the Youth Leadership Program took me to places that I never would have imagined. My team members and I were invited to public schools, community centres, individual homes, churches, and libraries to talk and conduct the program. I was able to help in starting over 30 Youth Leadership Programs during my time as a Youth Leadership Chair. This was an incredible learning experience for the coordinators, as well as the youth involved. I'm also pleased to say that over 400 youths experienced firsthand what the Youth Leadership program is all about. Someday, these youths will become powerful speakers in getting their message across, whether it is at home or in their careers. One of the unforgettable moments that my team and I shared was our visit to the children's hospital in Toronto, Ontario. We were invited to run a Youth Leadership Program workshop with the hospital's ambassadors.

It was heart-breaking to hear the speeches from these young kids who were diagnosed with major health problems. Even though they were very ill, they wanted to learn the art of public speaking, so they can spread awareness to others and fundraise for the cause. So far, the public speaking program has given me most of the tools and experience that I needed to grow as a great presenter in the public. This program has helped me grow my self-esteem and has allowed me to get acquainted with lots of people within my home club and overseas. There are many more opportunities and learning to gain from this program if you can think outside the box!

Work

WOW! I completed my 15 years of service on December 5, 2020, working at a Toronto hospital for the Psoriatic Arthritis Research Program as a Clinical Research Coordinator. I can vividly recall my first day on the job. At that time, everybody was planning on taking their time off for the holidays and I was already feeling that I was going to miss everyone. The first month was boring, but then after the holidays, everybody was back, and the fun and work started. After so many years this workplace had become like a second home. During lunch hour and after work, I started to connect with so many like-minded people and got involved with other activities. It was like being in high school, after the class is over then it is time for extracurricular activities, though I very much enjoyed my job too. There were up and down moments, but I think it is the greatest place to work. My favourite part was interacting with patients and explaining some of the research studies for them to participate in. I had the chance to work on some simple studies to some challenging recruitments. But overall, everything was for patient care. To be honest, the patient interaction is what kept me going for this long. Also, every year we had Fellows from around the world, summer students, and medical students, who came to our department to work on their projects. It always felt good to be able to be part of their success in some way, and it was a great feeling to see them succeed and complete their programs. Our workplace was not just about work. We had parties, celebrations for different occasions, and everybody was appreciated for their contribution to the program. It was a place where if you wanted to grow, there were opportunities. We were always trained to use the new technology that was available out there for our research studies, including websites and email communication with patients. I never got bored. Apart from that, since I love charity work, I got involved with the hospital's foundation.

I've organized bake sales, runs, or walks with my co-workers and friends to raise money on my own vacation time. With different activities, I was able to raise over $15, 000 to give to the fundraising campaign. This experience meant a lot to me and provided me with many life lessons, such as spirituality, friendship, care, kindness, and most of all, charity and helping others.

Volunteering Changed My Life

I was born and raised in Jaffna, Sri Lanka until the age of nine, when I was forced to leave my birthplace with my family to find a safer place to live, as the war was threatening our safety. My family and I fled and settled in Canada, which we are proud to call our home. I'm grateful every day for the life of freedom and opportunities that Canada has provided us, and, to this day, I give back through my volunteering, such as the food bank, shelters, charity events, and many more. I often reflect on when I was nine and feel compelled to help those who are in a similar situation in the world today.

Volunteering has brought so much joy to my life. The experience has brought me to so many different places and I have met so many people from all walks of life. You don't need to be rich to give back or make a difference in the world because anybody can make a difference. It doesn't matter how big or small the contribution, every little bit counts. You might not realize that a simple act of kindness – for example, helping someone with buying groceries, or spending some time with someone who needs the company – goes a long way. People often think that I have a lot of free time when I tell them that

I've been volunteering. I tell them: "It is not that I have all the time in the world to volunteer. If you truly want to make a difference in someone's life, you can make the time. It could be 10 minutes, 30 minutes, or one hour. When you see the smiles on the faces of the people you've helped, it makes you happy that you made a difference."

My Office "Mom"

Some people come into our lives and we don't know for what reason. However, as time goes by, we start to figure it out. My friend, Lisa, is one of those people and is a very special person in my life. I met her when I started my job at the hospital in 2005. She was working in the same department where I was hired, but a couple of years later, she moved to another department. Our friendship continued, with lunchtime chats, weekend phone calls, and going out together for events. Lisa has always treated me like her daughter. Lisa would support and encourage me with most of my activities, especially the marathons and a lot of my charitable events. She loved reading my public speaking program speeches and gave me feedback. She was one of those people who never missed saying "happy birthday" during all these years of friendship. She is a highly energized woman who retired in 2019 but still works one or two times a week. While she was working, she also pursued and completed her university studies in 2020. I was planning to attend her graduation, which was scheduled for the summer of 2020, but due to Covid-19, it didn't happen as an in-person event. Lisa was very dedicated and wanted to show her grandchildren that grandma is a graduate. I am so proud of Lisa for working so hard to get that degree, and I'm so happy for her!

Early on in our friendship, Lisa used to mention that I could have been her daughter, and we certainly have developed a strong family-like bond. It is so true that we don't know why some people come into our lives, whether it's for a long or short time, but with Lisa, I know I have a life-long friend.

My Fashion World

When I was young, I dreamed of wearing fancy dresses. I recall looking forward to watching the Oscars and seeing the beautiful gowns the actresses would wear. I would not miss a moment of it; you could say I was obsessed. I would imagine wearing those dresses myself and displaying them to an audience one day. My mom would tell me that I was wasting my time dreaming the impossible.

In 2020, I attended an event where volunteers were acknowledged for their services to the community. One of the ladies I met at this event was a fashion designer who had her own clothing line. After the award presentation, there was a fashion show with her models, which I truly enjoyed watching. Some of her attire fascinated me and felt I needed to tell her, so I introduced myself. Her name is Suzy Tamasy. Through our conversation, I learned that a portion of her proceeds from sales of her clothing goes to support a shelter for abused women. I felt a connection with Suzy immediately. I wanted to keep in contact with her, so the following day I sent her a message expressing how nice it was to meet her at the event. I told her how much I enjoyed her fashion show and admired what she does to help vulnerable women by supporting the women's shelter. I also wrote that I would love to be in her fashion show one day. A few days later, I got a message from Suzy and I was totally surprised! She asked me if I was interested in being a model for one of her fashion shows to raise money for the women's shelter. I responded right away with excitement! We met up in November 2020 and the show was set for February 2021. I recall counting down the days as I couldn't wait to participate, yet I didn't tell anyone about it. I was so excited to go and experience this moment that I had always dreamed of. Suzy told me that I could wear two different dresses for the fashion show. All her dresses were amazing and I was thrilled to walk the runway. Despite it being my first time, I was not nervous at all. I had an overwhelming feeling of happiness in me. The first round went well and then I waited for the second round. While I was waiting, I came across a few photographers who were taking pictures of the models. I had never been in an event that took so many photos. I snapped some shots of myself and posted them on my Facebook page while I was at the event. I was so surprised when I got home to see so many likes on my Facebook page. A week later, I attended an event and people asked me about the fashion show I had participated in. I felt important, almost famous. It boosted my confidence and I have become more interested in modelling since that day. Today, I have modelling photos in various magazines as a result of the opportunity Suzy gave me and I am so grateful.

Now, I reflect on those days when I use to watch the Oscars – how I looked at the beautiful gowns the actresses wore, and I how much I wanted to experience wearing a dress like that one day – and I can smile knowing that I was able to do what I once thought was unreachable! My dream came true!

The Art of Meditation

Peace of mind, happiness, and the joy of inner dialogue and self-awareness are the benefits that I've received by meditating. Going for walks after work for 15 minutes, 30 minutes, or one hour has given me a chance to explore different paths in the neighbourhood, as well as different locations with beautiful sceneries, buildings, people, stores, parks, and lakes. Over the many years, I have been able to connect and relax my mind this way. The power of meditation is hard to express in words; it can only be felt. Some people search for comfort and support from outside at times when they feel that they have hit rock bottom. I was on a personal journey, searching for a place where I would feel utterly at peace with myself and with the world when I stumbled upon the art of meditation. I think that there are several reasons why one may feel what I felt when I discovered the peace within. The moment one starts to look for answers within is the best way to allow meditation to occur naturally. We can feel the change within ourselves in unimaginable ways. All the time and dedication I've put toward meditation has created a mental pathway in my mind toward happiness and to look at things in different ways. The most amazing thing that others cannot miss is the glowing energy of a person who meditates and the positivity that individual spreads. They can feel the warmth in the presence of a person who does meditation regularly. The most important thing about meditation is that you will develop the skills to do it without any distraction. Once you discover the benefit of meditation, you do not feel the time pass. You will realize that there is so much to admire and enjoy the beauty of nature.

With my commitment and discipline toward meditation over many years, I have learned to keep away from negative thoughts, and my mind is at peace. I have also become calmer, stronger, more confident, and learned to face all the obstacles that I encountered. Meditation has shown me the right path to take whenever I am confused and the internal strength to persevere at times of difficulties. I have developed the ability to see the goodness in everyone. Once we realize that there is a greater power and when we respect that power, it is easier to see both our potential and beyond. Meditation practice has taught me the patience to wait for life's important lessons to happen at the time when they are supposed to happen.

Purpose and Gratitude

Life is always full of surprising events. There are things that we want to achieve and look forward to. Then there are things that we don't look forward to and it happens. There are also things that we want to happen but it never does. Each one of us on this planet is here for a purpose. As we grow up, we learn to understand our purpose and it comes with more experience and age. We go through so much in life – happy moments, sad moments, challenges, and learning experiences – all of which make us grow into the person we are destined to be. I am grateful for all the opportunities that life has given me. There were lots of happy moments and there were so many difficult times. I've realized that during our difficult times, we learn more about ourselves, appreciate what we already have, and not focus on what we don't have. I thank God for all the opportunities that I have been given over the years. I am grateful to have a wonderful family and friends, who care about me and support me during good and bad times. I'm also thankful to be part of this book as a co-author. It is always great to share and hear other women's empowering stories.

I would like to thank Suzy Tamasy for including me as one of the co-authors in this book. Most of all, I would like to thank Canada for giving me and my family a place to call home. I will always remember the day when my family and I had to leave our home and loved ones because of the Sri Lankan Civil War. Our life has changed so much since then. We lost our home, which was bombed during the war, and relatives and friends who migrated to other parts of the world. My family and I were lost when we landed in Canada as immigrants. But, to be honest, Canada is a country full of opportunities for people who are willing to put in the effort. I am forever grateful that I was able to complete my studies, and will never forget what this country has offered me – a peaceful place to call home, full of LOVE, LIGHT, PEACE & LAUGHTER.

Dedication

I am dedicating this book to my parents, who were the backbone of my future. They were brave to decide to leave their homeland, family, belongings, and the home that they worked hard to build. Their wishes were shattered when they had to leave everything behind, because of the escalating Sri Lankan Civil War in late 1985. They made this decision to save their children's lives from the deadly war. At that moment, they would not have thought of anything except safety. They did their best. We first landed in Denmark and stayed there for many years. We came to Canada afterward. I am so proud of my parents. They went through so many struggles, not knowing what the future would have held for their children.

I'm standing up to honour them, for managing to learn the language, adjusting to the new culture, and fitting in. Our house was bombed later when the civil war got worse.

Thank God we escaped. Since that day, I have felt grateful for everything I have in my life. I would like to thank my parents once again for making the biggest decision of their life for the future of their children and deciding to leave their country. Thank you to them for bringing sunshine into my life. Thank you to Denmark and Canada for giving us a safe place to live during our difficult time when my family was looking for a peaceful place.

I am lucky to have siblings who were there for me when I needed them, and I was there for them when they needed me. My brother was like a father figure to me. He understood more about me than my father did and has always been there throughout my life for any help and advice that I need. My sister has also been there for me on many occasions. We talk and share many things over the phone and in person to comfort each other through the difficult times and to enjoy fun times. I am also grateful to have wonderful nephews and a niece. I felt like a mother after having to babysit all three of them and felt blessed to have that opportunity.

I know that they will always think of me as a good aunt. I have learned many things from these kids. I become like a little kid too, when I spend my time with them. It is so fun to experience these moments through the eyes of the kids and what they make you do for their happiness. My family is well-known for cooking great meals. It started with my mom and whenever we had visitors, we always treated them to a good meal. I am so grateful to my siblings and sister-in-law, for always thinking about me and bringing over hot meals. I am never left without food; my fridge is always full.

I would like to thank my parents, brother, sister, Abinaash (Abi), Anjana, Jaswinth, sister-in-law, brother-in-law, and many great friends in my journey for their support. I would also like to thank Leonard Selvaratnam, Sutton Group Admiral Realty Inc., who is passionate to help seniors and people in need. I had a great chance to work with him over the past three years on some charitable events and got to know many people in the Tamil community through him. I would like to thank all these people and many others for their support.

Sutha Shanmugarajah

Back home

An Arranged Marriage

Volunteering made my Life

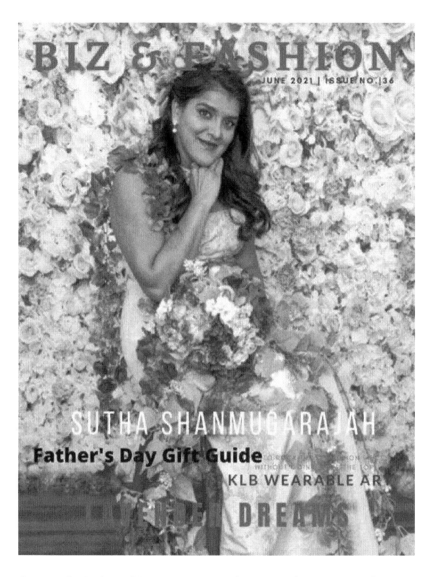

Cover of Biz & Fashion Magazine Photo credit Mario Mule
Dress design SQJ

At work

Walk in the woods photo credit Stan Trac wearing SQJ

Did Life Hand You Lemons? Let's Make Lemonade!

By Pat Kozyra

My contribution to this book, *Empowered in Heels,* will be laced with quotations, sayings, and expressions that may help to empower and inspire the women who read it. Of course, I realize there are many more ways to become inspired or motivated on our way to empowerment, but even if just one of these quotations rings a bell or hits home, it just may provide some impetus for you to act on something, or it may spark something in you to take action. "The purpose of life is a life of purpose!" I have a plaque with this engraved on it sitting on a shelf in my house.

I have also chosen to share many words of wisdom stemming from experiences in my life. This is the advice I would pass along to other women as a way to inspire, motivate, and empower. In life, we face many challenges, but I truly believe that when life hands you lemons, you should always try to make lemonade!

I'm Special (Author Unknown)

"I'm special. In all the world there is nobody like me. Since the beginning of time, there has never been another person like me. Nobody has my smile. Nobody has my eyes, my nose, my hair, my hands, my voice. I'm special. Nobody can be found who has my handwriting. Nobody anywhere has my tastes – for food or music or art. No one sees things just as I do. In all of time, there has been no one who laughs like me, no one who cries like me. And what makes me laugh and cry will never provoke identical laughter and tears from anybody else ever. No one reacts to any situation just as I would react; I'm special. I am the only one in all of creation who has my set of abilities.

Oh, there will always be someone who is better at one of the things I'm good at, but no one in the universe can reach the quality of my combination of talents, ideas, abilities, and feelings. Like a room full of musical instruments, some may excel alone but none can match the symphony sound when all are played together; I'm a symphony! Through all of eternity, no one will ever look, talk, walk, think, or do like me. I'm special. I'm rare. And, as in all rarity, there is great value. Because of my great value, I need not attempt to imitate others. I'll accept - yes, celebrate my differences. I'm special. And I am beginning to see that God made me special for a very special purpose. He must have a job for me that no one else can do as well as I. Out of all the billions of applicants, only one is qualified; only one has the right combination of what it takes. That one is ME, because... I'm special."

I think women should read this over to themselves often, and if they have children, I think *I'm Special* should be read to them at least once each school year. Children should be reassured that their parents realize that we all learn differently, at different rates, and with different learning styles. Remember it is said that "Popcorn is prepared in the same pot, over the same heat, and in the same oil, but they don't all POP at the same time. Don't compare yourself to others. Your turn to 'pop' is coming!"

It is no secret that I like and enjoy quotations. Many have meaningful and powerful messages, some can speak to us, or even help influence our thinking. If you were to have walked by my classroom or bulletin boards, you would have seen beautiful posters with inspiring quotations for students, parents, and teachers. For example: "It is nice to be important, but it is more important to be nice," or "A ship in the harbour is safe, but that is not what ships are for," or "To have a friend, you have to be a friend," or "Children must be taught how to think, not what to think."

I have friends and family who often ask me why I keep teaching and why I don't just stop and retire to simply enjoy life. I think the answer is that I truly do enjoy what I do and would not do it if I did not like it or gain some satisfaction from it or find it very rewarding. There is a saying: "Nothing in nature lives for itself. Rivers don't drink their own water. Trees don't eat their own fruit. The Sun doesn't shine for itself. Flowers don't spread fragrance for themselves. Living for others is the rule of Nature." It is rewarding to know that you have helped someone in a meaningful way.

Memories of My Father

My name is Patricia Yvonne Kozyra (nee Nykorchuk). I was seldom ever called Patricia, but I always liked reading the

Latin origin – words like noble, distinguished, or lofty birth and character. I never liked 'Patsy' and that was what I was called all through elementary school. I have no idea how that happened. The names Patty, Trish, and Trisha did not appeal to me either when people tried to address me with those names. When I entered high school, I pushed for just 'Pat,' and it somehow stuck. My middle name Yvonne means John in Ukrainian, and since I was born on my father's birthday, January 23rd, I can understand why that name was chosen. However, the story goes that my father had *really* wanted a boy at that time. My mother had lost twin boys shortly after their birth, even though they were at least five pounds each in weight. I was never told why, except that in those days it happened often, perhaps because of a lack of proper equipment. Next came my brother, whom my parents had 11 months before I was born. One of my aunts told me that my father was hoping to make up for the two lost boys. She told him, "Just wait, you will be proud of her someday!" I don't ever recall my dad saying that he was proud of me or any of my accomplishments, but when I think back there really weren't that many to boast about in those early days. He was a strict, serious father, and I was spanked a couple of times, though I never was punished the way my brother was with the leather belt. I would hide under the covers and try to plug my ears, crying just as loudly as he was. However, on my first day of teaching, I was sent a vase of flowers to the school with a card that said, "Congratulations from Dad," and that night I was asked for my first month of rent. I was crushed, to say the least, as I was hoping to buy a car before anything else, and never once thought about paying my parents' rent. When I got engaged, I was told they had saved all that money up for my wedding costs. I never had much luck with cars. The first one I ordered, a white Valiant with red upholstery, got smashed on the ship carrying it, so that was the end of that. The red Volkswagen that I finally settled on, caught fire from the gas heater while I was driving it, and apparently, my insurance had expired, so another lesson was learned about attention to detail. My dad had several cars and kindly gave me one to drive. Here is what someone said about our fathers: "If after you are grown and think back on your father and your childhood, and you smile, then you were raised by a great man." My dad was often very helpful when I needed him after I became an adult, like the night he took the pipes apart under the sink to find my contact lens, or the night his big heavy vehicle was able to drive us in a blizzard to the hospital when our daughter broke her arm. Of course, my birthday each year now without him, has me recalling the birthdays we shared together.

"Always a bridesmaid, never a bride!"

As a small child, I often wished I could be a real flower girl at a wedding, but that never happened, so the book called *Junie B. Jones is Almost a Flower Girl* by Barbara Park, is one of my favorites. I remember the first two weddings I attended as a young child with my parents like it was yesterday. I was a real bridesmaid at three weddings: my brother's and two of my girlfriends.

Throughout my life, I have had many disappointments of not quite hitting the mark or not being the winner (being the bridesmaid and not the bride, so to speak). Some of those moments include the time I came second in a speech competition in Grade Eight, never winning in any piano festival competitions, losing the position of Phys. Ed Coordinator because a check of my documents showed one of the courses was not entirely applicable to the position, or not winning a prestigious award for my book. What these experiences have taught me is that we while may not always win at life, there are always other chances to excel, and that even the disappointing moments can teach us valuable lessons.

On Living with Regrets

I regret not laughing enough or having enough to laugh about, and I am not even sure if I smile enough. I think as a child I had a very embarrassing high-pitched cackle which must have bothered many. I always say how much I miss my dear friend, Celine, in Thunder Bay because we would laugh at so many things when we were together. I like this quote about friendship: "Laughter and compassion are two vital building blocks of friendship, but loyalty is the cement that seals the bond."

I regret not tape recording or videotaping my parents long before they died, so that I, along with my daughters and grandchildren, could hear their voices, see them, and listen to their answers to questions. I wish I had asked them because now I *really* want to know the answers, and it is too late. My husband, Taras wrote his life story into five beautiful hard-covered books a few years ago to hand down to our children and grandchildren, but it dawned on us that few students today learn or use cursive writing, so Naomi, my book marketing consultant, videotaped him reading the entire works and stored it on USBs.

I regret not attending my grade nine piano examination because I was too afraid that I would fail or felt too unprepared. I am surprised that my parents did not make me go to try it anyway, and just do my best. I know I disappointed my piano teacher who had worked so hard to prepare me. Years later, long after Teacher's College, I attended university with the intent of getting a degree. Yes, I did take a piano course and did quite well in it. I had to dig all those grade nine piano books out of my parents' basement where they were stored in boxes.

I regret not being able to say goodbye at the death bed of some very special people in my life, and not just because I was not living near them, but because I was totally unequipped as to what to say, how to say it, and how to handle myself there.

I regret not looking after my health better in so many ways over the years. Here is an example (Side note – my husband and I lived in Hong Kong where I was a teacher for many years): When I left Hong Kong, I was discharged from Queen Mary Hospital after spending 10 days there with a life-threatening condition that I was unaware of and unprepared for. It is all like a big nightmare now!

On September 24th, I woke up with my left arm, hand, and fingers in full paralysis with little or no use for most of that day. When I finished teaching my last student that night, I went to the emergency room at the hospital. They concentrated on checking my brain for a suspected stroke, with their focus being on the CT scan and MRI for verification. However, these all turned out to be completely normal, so thinking it was just a one-off thing and noticing that much of my feeling was slowly being restored that night at the hospital, they sent me home but said they would do some blood tests. I left and was ready to finish the massive task of packing and sorting all the teaching materials before the movers came.

 To my surprise, the phone began ringing after midnight and when I answered, it was the hospital telling me it was very urgent and to get myself back there immediately. It was only at this point that I revealed the diet plan I had stupidly put myself on without any doctor consultation or advice. This was not a wise decision. I had seen an interview with a celebrity who talked about losing 100 pounds on a certain program of capsules, along with a couple of other homemade concoctions of supplements; in desperation, I decided to give it a try on my own. However, with so many pre-existing conditions, especially the inherited autoimmune disease called Hashimoto's Disease that manifests itself late in life, this plan was so very wrong for my body, and I did not know how dangerous it was! In two months or so, I had lost nearly 30 pounds, but was always very thirsty and had terrible leg cramps each night. I had no idea I was poisoning myself, and my condition was life-threatening.

It was so fortuitous that our first scheduled flight through Vancouver was cancelled due to Covid-19 (amongst the crew members, apparently). The doctors questioned if I would have even made it to Canada, so I feel very lucky for that cancelled flight, and so fortunate to have had such wonderful doctors and nurses at the hospital caring for me. The first thing I did after I was released was to go to church to thank God that I was still here, and to sing the whole mass for the very last time before leaving. What an emotional time! I could see from where I was up at the altar that Tara's was crying through much of the mass, thankful I think, that it was not my funeral. We got our next flight on Oct 11, one day before the big typhoon, and returned to our life in Canada. I am slowly adjusting to a completely new lifestyle. Unfortunately, some of the drugs from Hong Kong were not available in Canada but I was fortunate to find a family doctor who would take me on, and an endocrinologist who has truly taken charge of my condition and found substitute medications.

I regret that I was not interested enough, nor did I take more part in our financial investments or managing our money. (I think this should be a mandatory course to take in high school!) Perhaps I could have effected some change in how we handled money – more like mishandled – throughout our marriage if I had asserted myself more and was proactive.

I regret being separated from our children and grandchildren for such long periods of time during the 20 years we were in

Hong Kong. I'm not sure the money we made there compensated for this enough or at all, even though it helped them out at times financially, afforded them nice holidays, and paid off their student loans.

I regret that I was not able to be at my father's bedside when he died. I was flying back to Hong Kong when he was taken to hospital from his old age home. When the plane landed in Hong Kong, I got the news of his death and returned to Canada immediately. I was thankful to my brother's wife, Clara, for dealing with and taking charge of so many aspects of moving my father from the family home while we were in Hong Kong.

"Life throws us curves! Accept what is, let go of what was, and have faith in what will be."

That brings me to one more regret, which is foolishly thinking I could solve our money problems by starting up two stores called *Exclusive Leather Fashions*, and *The Gift Basket*. I was teaching full-time, teaching Special Education courses at the university, and somehow trying to raise two children. I stupidly hitchhiked on an idea of the beautiful gift basket store I saw in Toronto. I did not do research, had little money for overhead costs and store rental, had no business sense, no networking to learn from, or even to find out how and where to buy things wholesale. I only acted on an idea and a whim.

I had trouble with staffing (one part-time girl, unfortunately, suffered from epilepsy which was problematic), was exhausted working the evening shifts, my brother was not happy about his wife giving of her time to work there, and it all came crashing down after only one year. I tell students all the time to "run with your strengths." Operating two stores was not one of my strengths, to say the least!

I regret that I sometimes criticize my husband or others for mistakes that I make as well, and that sure teaches me a lesson.

A *Tiny Buddha* quote I read once says: "We all have a past. We've all made choices that maybe weren't the best ones. None of us are completely innocent, but we get a fresh start every day to be a better person than we were yesterday."

"The only thing we have to fear is fear itself." ~ Franklin Roosevelt

I have a real fear of not accomplishing, experiencing, or completing all the things in my life that I set out in my mind to do. For that reason, I hate birthdays now more than ever and wish I could turn back the clock because they remind me that I may not have that much time left.

I'm afraid of our house burning down again. One time, my father filled a pot-bellied stove with too much wood, and it exploded and burned our house to the ground. He was able to throw one trunk out of the window and that was all that was saved. It contained our baby books, our Christening gowns, and my mother's embroidery pieces which I still have today. I can remember watching children on their way to school come by, sifting the ashes in hopes of finding some money or little treasures. For years I had an escape plan with my best dolls and toys ready to jump out the window if this should ever happen again.

I always feared sickness, or my mother being ill. I feared drunk men, so much so, that I was afraid to pass a man on the road while walking home from school, and once in the winter I took a detour through a field to avoid such an encounter and got stuck in the ice and snow. A neighbour saw from her window and got out of her sickbed to pull me out. My father used to often say, "Stop crying or I will give you something to cry about!" My mother said when she went for an interview with my high school English teacher, he told her I seem to worry a lot. Taras has little patience or tolerance for it and shows little empathy or sympathy. He says he is just trying to toughen me up more, and that I worry needlessly about many things, read too much into a situation, and analyze incorrectly what people will think. Sophia Bush said, "I just wish I hadn't spent so much time worrying about not being someone else's enough." I worry about whether I was a good enough mother, whether I might have hurt someone's feelings, whether the house is clean enough, about all Taras' past and present ailments or illnesses, about travelling on a plane, about our debts, about our children and grandchildren, and the list goes on.

Vex King said: "Instead of telling people that they shouldn't feel a certain way, try understanding why they feel that way. Don't invalidate how THEY feel because YOU don't agree with it. You can learn so much about other people and inspire compassion if you're willing to listen."

On Beliefs and Convictions

For a variety of reasons, I have come to believe in the following: the power of prayer, karma, serendipity, ghosts, spirit guides, archangels, guardian angels who send us signs, The Law of Attraction, self-actualization, visualization, dreams that have meanings and messages, that trees have feelings, aliens, astrology, meditation, reincarnation, past life regression, and the fact that there are no coincidences in life. "Everything happens for a reason. That reason causes change. Sometimes it hurts. Sometimes it's hard, but in the end, it's all for the best."

Let me tell you a true story about coincidence: While looking for a tattered coat for the character playing the wizard in *The Wizard of Oz*, a costume assistant bought one from a second-hand store. When the actor put the coat on, he turned the pocket inside out, and written in the pocket was the name L. Frank Baum, the author of *The Wizard of Oz* books. Baum's widow later identified the coat as actually having belonged to

225

her husband. In high school, we heard of twin brothers who were each adopted by a different family, and they discovered each other by accident in university. It is said we meet everyone for a reason, and they are either a blessing or a lesson.

I also believe in divine intervention, spirits of departed souls of our friends and family helping us, praying for us, guiding us, warning us, and even counselling us. I believe those stories of returning to Earth from a near-death experience, having passed to the other side with the light at the end of the tunnel, and I believe that there are human representations of evil here on Earth. I believe in the concept of heaven and hell, spirituality, following your intuition, which is your inner guidance. I believe in psychic ability and each time I visit a psychic I am told I also have that gift. I believe in gut feelings, unexplained miracles, signs from the divine that come to guide us through feathers or flickering lights. I believe people who say they have received messages or signs and signals from their loved ones who have passed on. If I am perceived as a gullible person, I can live with that, no problem. My husband is terribly afraid of swimming/water/the ocean, and he could tell both serious and humorous stories on that topic, but the interesting thing I learned when I visited a renowned past-life regressionist in Toronto, was that she saw that my husband, in one of his many past lives, was a sea captain who went down with the ship in a storm. Makes sense to me!

Taras and I have both come to believe that we have encountered real, true-life angels here on Earth several times since we left Hong Kong. It started when we met John and Carmen at church and found out they were moving to Canada as well. They spent many hours converting all my computer hard drive material onto USBs so I could leave the computer for my helper to send to her children in the Philippines. Angels for sure.

When I was discharged from the hospital and went to pay the bill for the 10 days, we got very lost as the stall had been shut down. As we stood there perplexed about what to do or where to turn next, a woman appeared out of nowhere and offered to help us. She accompanied me the whole time as it was very difficult to find, stood in line with me, shared that she was a diabetic, ran to a convenience store to make sure I had crackers and sugar candy in my purse, walked with me the whole way back to the prescription room where Taras was waiting, and kept refusing the $100 I put in her pocket as she ran off to go home. She wished us well as she shouted, "My name is Milly!" We believe Milly was another real-life angel.

One night in Oshawa, my phone was out of charge and my device died. It was a holiday and I needed it for my Zoom teaching the next morning. The only store open was a drug store and the clerk there looked high and low for one, but they were sold out. He used his own to test mine and said yes, I needed a new one. While talking to him I had mentioned that I had just gotten my second vaccine. Then he said that he wanted me to have his own device as a congratulatory gift for getting my second Covid shot. Can you imagine my joy and surprise!? That clerk was a real-life angel.

We also consider my daughter   Tana, and son-in-law Joel, who have handled almost every aspect of our lives since we landed in Canada, along with our multitude of problems and challenges - real-life angels as well. Tana negotiated the buying of our house with such skill and expertise during the bidding wars, even though she too, was dealing with a major illness. Added to that was the help and support of our daughter Tara, Tim, and children who travelled from London, Ontario to pitch in and assist us.

"Pet peeves should be kept on a leash." ~ Daniel Thompson

I don't have much patience with people who are late for appointments, do not apologize for it, make up excuses each time, and do not call to say they will be late. I hate being accused of something I absolutely did not do or say. Something that *really* bothers me is people who wear big full bulging backpacks onto the airplane with no regard for the people they bump and hit, or even injure, as they walk down the aisle – there should be a rule about that! It is quite unbelievable nowadays observing families in restaurants who ignore each other the whole time, only look at their phones and gadgets, and pay for the meals that they or their kids did not even touch.

And then there are "fair weather friends," those so-called good friends who suddenly do not have your back when you are sick, lonely, sad, or need financial help. It has taken me far too long to learn this: "Stop swimming across the ocean for someone who would not even jump over a mud puddle for you." I guess that is what loving yourself more is all about; when you love yourself, you attract better. You let the universe know that you deserve the best by treating yourself well. Everything starts with how you feel about yourself. Feel worthy, feel valuable, feel special, feel deserving of receiving the best. Feel it in your heart and you will attract it. Someone once said, "The best thing about the worst times of your life is that you get to see the true colours of everyone."

The last pet peeve that I will mention is about communication. Some of my friends tell me that they talk to their children at least once or twice a day. I feel sad that we did not have a better plan or system worked out with our daughters and grandchildren to keep in touch more often. This quote is a good one: "A little communication goes such a long way. If you're busy, say it. If you're upset, express it.

If you're running late, let people know; If you don't want to do something, be straightforward. If you're unsure, ask. It's so simple, but so important."

On Experiences that Make Me Proud and Grateful

I am proud of my children, their spouses, and our six grandchildren for so many reasons, even though a mother never stops worrying about them. "A mother's dream is to see her kids supporting each other and being best friends long after she is gone."

I am proud of how I coped in life with all its challenges. I am proud of my successes in education and how I have helped so many students to achieve and become successful contributors to society. I am proud of my husband for overcoming so many obstacles in his life as a refugee from Ukraine, as a child struggling to learn a new language in his new country, Canada, and as an educator, a politician, and a public servant.

I am proud of the fact that I learned how to communicate a bit in Ukrainian with Auntie Paraska when she arrived in Canada, not knowing how to speak English, to babysit our children. We both kept it a secret, as I was too embarrassed to let any other family members hear me speak. Her life story is one for another book. I was so proud of her learning how to put in contact lenses that gave her some sight. She is so sadly missed.

I am thankful for the brilliant doctor from England, who took care of our first daughter, Tara, when after being bitten by mosquitos, suffered from "Skin Scald Syndrome" and nearly died. This doctor knew how to treat it successfully.

I am so thankful for the many good friends I still have now and have had over the years, who continue to offer support, and give sage advice or cautions; the friends whom I can laugh with, travel with, and at times agree to disagree. We know the meaning of friendship.

I am thankful for my observant nature and my good memory thus far (even though both of my parents died with Alzheimer's

Disease, and while a test is available to see if I too will meet that fate, I have chosen not to be tested and will take my chances with not knowing).

Taras and I laugh now at the fact that it sometimes takes the two of us to remember something. Now I understand why someone wrote: "I've finally reached the Wonder Years – Wonder where I parked the car? Wonder where I left my phone? Wonder where my glasses are? Wonder what day it is?"

I am proud that I like to help people, share what I have with them, give of myself, and go out of my way for those I really care about, or who truly need help. We once overheard a family with three children in a restaurant in total angst as there were no hotel rooms available that night because of a big convention being held in the city. We brought them all to our home that night and became very good friends for years after, and they hosted us many times at their home in Toronto.

I am proud of the fact that I bought a palette and oil paints for a native student I was teaching when I discovered his unbelievable talent and even prouder when I attended an exhibit of his artwork years later.

I am proud of taking the "bull by the horns" with courses for speaking when I finally decided to learn the techniques of conquering my real fear of speaking in front of people (for example, even asking or answering a question at a staff meeting without memorizing it in my mind first and with my heart pounding).

I am proud to have received the John E. Weaver Excellent Read Award 2017 as the winner for Non-Fiction Education from Earthshine Media Group.

I am proud of both my daughters for their entrepreneurial spirit and for taking strong initiative with opportunism. They have never been afraid to try new things and embark on new adventures, and I can see these fine qualities in every one of our six grandchildren, each with unique talents and abilities.

I am also proud of my YouTube channel called *Read Me a Story by Pat Kozyra*, where I sing and read over 120 books to children whose parents cannot read them a bedtime story because they do not speak English, and grateful for the assistance from my very capable book marketing consultant, Naomi Chui, who filmed all those book-reading sessions. (We met in a Starbucks by accident – or was it really?) Another real-life angel!

I am proud that I, as a Catholic, had the courage and willingness to accept a teaching position in a Jewish School and was able to learn so much about the Jewish faith, culture, and language. I can sing the Hebrew national anthem and recite some prayers by heart, no problem!

I am proud that I can be as positive about life as I am. Amy Weatherly said, "Some people could be given an entire field of roses and only see the thorns in it. Others could be given a single weed and only see the wildflower in it. Perception is a key component of gratitude. And gratitude is a key component to joy." I think I am a strong person not only physically, but also courageously. My parish priest told me during confession once, to always say a prayer for those who have offended you or hurt you, which is not always easy. Ziad Abdelnour said,

"Never blame anyone in your life. The good people give you happiness. The bad people give you experience. The worst people give you a lesson. The best people give you memories."

"Above all else, embrace your flaws." ~ JH Hard

Counting my chickens before they are hatched, so to speak, is one of the worst things I have done so often in life, and it can result in such disappointment, low self-esteem, frustration, and even anger – especially if I am so excited that something will happen or manifest itself, and I even announce it to others prematurely.

Another fault is my multi-tasking that experts say has no positive results or benefits whatsoever and it drives my husband bananas.

When he asks me to watch a movie with him, I might bring a book, my phone, and at the same time, soak my feet, mend, or attend to my nails. Amy Weatherly wrote: "Hey you! You're holding onto too many bags. You can't do it all. You can't be it all. You can't carry it all. Do what you can. Be who you are. Only carry what's important. And put the rest of the bags down!" I also think that at times I have a lack of patience and attention span, should be a better listener, and should not criticize until I have walked in someone else's shoes. A senior citizen said, "When you are frustrated with me because of the things I cannot do, just imagine how frustrated I must be because I'm no longer able to. So, be mindful and show compassion." I am learning this more and more now as my husband and I realize the limits to certain things we used to be able to do so well and so easily. Does getting old suck? Yes, at times it *really* does!

John Lennon once said, "Life is what happens to you when you're making other plans." Now that we are back from Hong Kong after 20 years, and had to make the difficult choice of where to live in the final phase of our life – in Ontario near our children and grandchildren, or at our holiday home in the Canary Islands – I always remember friends of ours telling us never pull up stakes just to move next to your children because you never know when they will have to or want to up pick stakes and also move for some reason or another. We are crossing our fingers on that one! We chose Ontario!

My Thoughts About Prayer

"Do not pray for an easy life but pray instead to be a strong person." They say that God does not give us anything we cannot handle, and I often think of that. Sometimes I look up there and ask, "God, are you testing me yet again?" I think that many times our prayers are so focused on asking for something, wanting something, or needing something, that we forget to say, "thank you" for bringing us this far, for helping us to say the right thing, to do the right thing, and to be the right "thing." If guardian angels/spirit guides/friends and family members who have passed on are helping us and watching over us, then the "thank you" should be extended there as well. I often remind myself of that.

Working Toward My Future

I long to resume my solo singing work, not only at a church but also singing again at weddings, funerals, and other events. I would also be willing to hold gatherings for women's groups wanting to share and network with positive ideas, positive thoughts, positive advice, and have ample opportunity to laugh and learn.

Since my husband and I were not yet ready to retire in Canada where our teaching careers had begun in the early 1960s, and we both wanted to continue working in the field of education, we decided to leave Canada in 2001 and went to Hong Kong. There, I continued my career as a learning specialist, nursery teacher, Pre-K teacher, Head of Preschool, Grade One teacher, music teacher, and private tutor, and my husband as Senior English Specialist, Evaluator of Teachers at the Faculty of Education in Hong Kong, Vice Principal of the Korean International School, Principal of the Korean International School, Senior English (part-time) at Victoria Shanghai Academy, and private tutor. Neither of us had to advertise for private students as it was all word of mouth. We were indeed lucky!

My Book: *Tips and Tidbits for Parents and Teachers*

The idea of writing a book struck me when I was preparing to throw out all my materials, resources, and books which I had saved during my teaching career.

I wanted to glean and share the best bits of tips and valuable knowledge I had learned and put it together into a book. Why? Because during my 50 years in the classroom, it became more and more apparent that parents *really* needed help in assisting with their child's education to meet individual needs successfully. Also, in working with, and helping not only student teachers, but colleagues as well, I felt and was convinced by others, that many could benefit from my book, and so I decided to act on this.

All parents want their child to become a productive contributor to society someday, and most parents are doing the very best they can. But sometimes it isn't enough, and this is where I come in. My book does just that – it helps parents.

My book begins with dos and don'ts right off the bat that I feel all parents should know – no if's, and's, or but's – I did not beat around the bush with this chapter. It tells what I have observed, what I know to be true, and what works and what doesn't work with children.

One example? You are not your child's best friend – you are your child's parent, and many parents forget this and are even afraid to be a parent.

I have included simple diagnostic tests and checklists that parents can give to their children to assess and test a wide variety of abilities right at home quickly and easily.

Having taught gifted children in Canada for 15 years before I went to Hong Kong, the chapter in my book on Giftedness is a big one. I often gave workshops on Giftedness for both parents and teachers, as well as a one-hour webinar presentation called *How Parents Can Help Their Child at Home* in October 2014, which can be found on the web or by contacting me.

I am the mother of two daughters and the grandmother of six delightful grandchildren all here in Ontario, so I come well qualified to talk about topics such as discipline, self-esteem, how to study for tests and exams, or even how to deal with things such as head lice, sleepovers, and birthday parties. It's all there in my book! You will also learn about the seven worst things that good parents do.

One chapter many parents tell me they are so happy to see in my book is the one explaining all the educational terms and vocabulary used on report cards and assignments for students.

Parents are often so frustrated with the language used, many are not familiar with the jargon, and are often too embarrassed to have it explained by the teacher. It is my strong opinion that many report cards today are very difficult to understand, and not even helpful to parents. Some are just downright ridiculous with so much educational jargon cutting and pasting from official documents, and at times not even describing the child accurately.

Some parents say the most enlightening chapter in my book is the one about Gender Differences. I express very strong opinions in my book about such things as chronic sleep deprivation, sleepovers, playdates, the role of the helper in your home, extracurricular activities, after-school tutoring lessons, and yes, homework. Now, if I ever have an administrative role again (perhaps in my next life), the only homework that would be assigned at my school would be reading, playing, and activities for families to do together. When is the last time you and your family played board games or read together in a quiet living room setting? This is called modelling for children. My husband and I both notice how students and even their parents are so much more stressed in recent years. The bar seems to be set so high now, and we notice this stress comes in the form of anxiety, body tics, and even full-blown Tourette's Syndrome.

The last chapter of my book is full of motivational and inspirational entries that will touch your heart for sure! The book concludes with a couple of letters from former gifted students, who, after 30 years, have tracked me down on social media. These letters contain some very surprising revelations, and I was thrilled to receive them. An example is one that came from Fawn Fritzen, a jazz soloist from Yukon (Album – Bedroom Voice).

I am proud of my book, as well as the many articles geared mainly toward parents that I have written as a freelance writer for *SCMP*, *The Epoch Times*, the prestigious *STEM Magazine* in U.S., and magazines such as *Sassy*, *Parent Guide*, and *Playtimes*, to name a few.

Inspiring Women

When we first arrived back in Canada from Hong Kong in October of 2020, we hunkered down in my daughter's basement apartment for six months, avoiding the Covid-19 pandemic and looking for somewhere to live. My daughter, who is a real estate agent, naturally took charge of trying to find us a place, and as our luck would have it, the decision to move here coincided with the price for homes escalating beyond belief. Sadly, we were forced to sell our holiday home in the Canary Islands to financially help solve this shocking situation with almost every house ending up in bidding wars, and home inspections became a thing of the past.

So, once we moved in, the monumental task of unpacking began, which included two shipments – one from the Canary Islands and one from Hong Kong. While unpacking, I happened to discover a small, tattered book that lost all its coils and was published in 1995 by Great Quotations Publishing Company. It was compiled by Patricia Martin. Surprisingly to me, it was printed in Hong Kong! This book was dedicated to her women friends who had enriched her life in countless ways. Sadly, though, I do not recall who gifted me with this little treasure. It is called *Words from Great Women* and Martin says she chose these remarkable women for their wisdom, wit, and piercing perceptions which are timeless, poignant, and thought-provoking. Let's learn from them and be empowered by their wisdom. I have chosen different ones to share with you to whet your appetite for more at your leisure. Enjoy!

Anne Frank: (from her Diary) – "In spite of everything, I still believe that people are really good at heart."

"We all live with the objective of being happy; our lives are all different and yet the same."

Eleanor Roosevelt: "A woman is like a teabag. You never know how strong she is until she gets into hot water."

Georgia O'Keefe: "The days you work best are the best days."

"I feel there is something unexplored about women that only a woman can explore."

Harriet Beecher Stowe: "Women are the architects of society. Most mothers are instinctive philosophers."

Helen Keller: "Life is either a daring adventure or nothing."

Maya Angelou: "Pursue the things you love doing, and then do them so well that people can't take their eyes off you." (From her book, *I Know Why the Caged Bird Sings*)

Gloria Steinem: "Self-esteem isn't everything; it's just that there's nothing without it."

Virginia Woolf: "Anything may happen when womanhood has ceased to be a protected occupation."

Oprah Winfrey: "When I look into the future it is so bright it burns my eyes."

"Luck is a matter of preparation meeting opportunity."

Mother Teresa: "We can do no great things. Only small things with great love."

"Kind words can be short and easy to speak, but their echoes are truly endless."

Inspiration From Famous People

So often in my life, I have turned to books first to help me along the way with solving issues and problems. I very much enjoy biographies and autobiographies, perhaps because I learn that other people go through similar, and sometimes much worse, things in their lives, meet these challenges, survive, and thrive. I also learn how lucky I truly am, and it helps me to be very thankful. That is why we called them "self-help" books.

The following famous people who have shared their unbelievable life stories and whom I believe are truly worth the read are: Nelson Mandela, Oprah Winfrey, Dolly Parton, Jane Fonda, Marie Osmond, Shania Twain, Celine Dion, Marlo Thomas, Jennifer Lopez, and of course, Debbie Reynolds!

When I was in high school, I secretly wanted to become an actress! One day, I decided to write a letter to Debbie Reynolds. I never shared this with my parents or brother for fear of being laughed at. My mother had bought me the sheet music for the song, "Tammy" and I sang it and played it on the piano hundreds of times. I wrote a letter to Debbie Reynolds and surprisingly she replied in length to answer my questions about becoming an actress. Fast forward to a family trip to Las Vegas years later with Taras and our two teenage daughters Tara and Tana, where we stayed at the hotel that Debbie Reynolds owned and housed her famous museum with collections of memorabilia items from the movies. She also performed there each night. Armed with her autobiography to get signed, and the very letter she wrote to me, we attended her show. It was miraculously arranged by her son, Todd, for her to meet me after the show, sit down, chat, take pictures, and present the letter to her. What a wonderful and memorable experience!

While I am on the topic of famous people, looking back now at my life, I fully realize not everyone gets the chance or opportunity to meet and greet a famous person. Here are some that I've had the privilege and thrill to meet:

- When Taras was a member of the city council, we met Queen Elizabeth and Prince Philip during their visit to Thunder Bay. We thoroughly studied the 10 or 12 pages of 'rules' we had previously received – what to say, what not to say, how to curtsey, what to wear, what not to wear, what to give, what not to give, and so on. The meeting was an outdoor event on a very windy day. All the members of the council and their spouses stood in a long line. When she came down the row to Taras, a loud jet plane soared overhead and he could not hear her question to him, and so he was forced to say, "I beg your pardon, Your Majesty.

What she had asked was what he did for a living outside of the council work. My eyes were glued the whole time on that purple brooch she wore on her right shoulder. I still have the white crotched gloves I wore that day and have never washed them since.

- Another pleasure was meeting Sarah Ferguson and Prince Andrew at Old Fort William. I had a lovely chat with her while we gathered inside for hors d'oeuvres. I still have the children's book she wrote called *Little Red*.

- I was very proud to meet Betty, the mother of Terry Fox when she visited Thunder Bay after his monument was completed. She had contributed a recipe in his honour to a Celebrity Cookbook that one of my gifted classes had created as a fundraiser for a charity. She told me it was Terry's favorite dessert (with Rice Krispies).

What fun my class had receiving recipes from famous people and having their letters responded to. The most exciting was the day my student walked into my classroom with a big white envelope with a gold seal from Buckingham Palace. The spokeswoman had written a thank you and an apology that she could not give a recipe out but that the Queen loved kiwi, so she could choose a recipe on her behalf instead. The most important thing about this is that the class had laughed and mocked this student for choosing to write to the Queen, saying that she would never get a reply, and how stupid a choice she had made. I cannot tell you what we all learned from that!

Women in Politics

At one point in my life, as I became more and more ensconced in my husband's political life, I also had considered running for a political position myself. (Taras was a member of the City Council for 20 years in Thunder Bay, Ontario, and a Liberal MPP in Ontario for three years, which ended when the Liberal Government under the leadership of David Peterson was ousted for calling an election too early). I was very involved in the Women's Associations of the Liberal Party both Provincially and Federally. I opened my home to countless meetings and political gatherings. Even though some psychics I visited could see success for me in that endeavour, for several reasons, it was not meant to be and never happened. Looking back on it now, I feel like I dodged a bullet! All I had to do was realize how much it turned off my husband from politics once he got there; when he found out how things are *really* run, what you have to do to get a cabinet post, how much back-stabbing there is, and how it disrupts family life and the marriage. If you think an MPP makes a ton of money, I have news for you! There were times when those cheques from the government just did not arrive in time to cover all the expenses – travel costs, apartment rental, campaigning costs, grocery/food/restaurant costs – we were eventually so deep in debt after Taras lost in that election that was called early, we decided to rent out the spare bedrooms our own girls had vacated when they left the nest. We chose female teacher's college students, and of course, we were able to assist them immensely in their studies. It was not

241

entirely without some stress and tension when our girls came home for the holidays.

There were times I did not want to walk down the street for fear of being stopped by business owners who would politely say that they had not yet received their money for something or other.

Campaigning for my husband door-to-door, handing out brochures, as any supportive wife would naturally do, was not easy.

I would come home in tears, unable to endure the nasty comments about the Premier calling an early election, and how they would send him a message and oust the Liberals. After losing the election, it was very difficult for Taras to get his teaching position back. People do not think of these scenarios when they run initially and think they have earned a spot to eventually receive a good pension from the Government upon retirement. You must serve many years to qualify for that. It was difficult to have virtually no family life during the weekdays when he was is sitting in Parliament, or the minute he got off the plane on a Friday night it meant he was off to a banquet, social gathering, or political gathering of some sort. What often upset and angered me was the fact that I could not even tell my husband any important news of the day or week because they seldom sit the wife next to the MPP at these functions. She is always next to a stranger at another table.

On Saturdays, he would rush off to his local office to troubleshoot there all morning, take all the calls, answer any concerns, and try to solve the issues presented to him. When that was over, he was off to a 50th anniversary or a 100th birthday party to hand the person a plaque from the Prime Minister, Premier, or the Queen. Then there was the night when his plane could not land due to a big blizzard, and hundreds of people were waiting for him to speak at Finn Hall.

So, who do you think had to fill in for him? The wife! Thank God, they loved me! Why? Because I look very Finnish. They all assumed that I was Finnish, too, and were surprised when I wasn't answering their questions in that language as well. In fact, they told me to tell my husband to send me next time, so we got a big laugh out of that for sure.

I need not tell you about Sunday because, you guessed it – Taras would fly back to Toronto and I would go back to the classroom on Monday. That was our week and it seldom varied.

For any women itching to throw their hat into the political ring, I will share with you some insight I gave in a short speech that I delivered in Toronto in the mid-nineties for the Liberal Women's Commission.

In plain and simple language, it is not easy for women to be in politics. With the help of surveys, statistics, interviews, and insights from women politicians, you will see not only how daunting and formidable a career choice this can be, but also why it is very important to encourage more women to become involved in politics.

It has often been said that Parliament Hill is a male bastion: the untouched world of 'male' privilege and influence, and women are not comfortable in those surroundings playing by those rules. If you don't look tough, you don't have what it takes. However, it has been said that the presence of women has already changed the complexion, tone, and nature of the debates in parliament, and that is good!

Women are an important element in parliament because they show high energy levels, good leadership ability, good common sense, and they are usually there for the right reasons. They commit to the task, and they get things done with a follow-through approach. Women are very capable of transcending partisan politics.

Women are slowly paving the way for more women to be encouraged to run. They feel they are good role models, and that more work would be accomplished in the areas of social problems, childcare, social justice, poverty, and environmental issues. Finally, on a positive note, most women in politics feel it is an incredible honour and duty to serve in such a way, and they feel they had truly contributed in that they had influenced policy issues.

"There will always be a reason why you meet people. Either you need them to change your life, or you're the one who will change theirs." ~ Angel Floris Harefa

Some parting words as I come to the end of my story. I want to share a quote I once read on the Higher Perspectives Facebook page: "There is a purpose for everyone you meet. Some come into your life to test you, some to teach you, some to use you, and some to bring out the very best in you. Those that bring out the best in us are the ones to bring us positive changes. They are the sunshine people that we'd want to spend time with, grow, explore, and make amazing memories."

By meeting me in this book, I hope that I have been one of those 'sunshine' people.

Just remember what Italian actress Sophia Loren once said: "Mistakes are part of the dues one pays for a full life."

Zig Ziglar once said, "A great attitude becomes a great mood, which becomes a great day, which becomes a great year, which becomes a great life!"

Enjoy that lemonade!

Dedication

I tried to think of someone other than my mother to dedicate this writing to, because I had already dedicated my own book to her in 2013, called *Tips and Tidbits for Parents and Teachers: Celebrating 50 Years in the Classroom and Sharing What I Have Learned,* but each time I thought about all those things that can empower women, my mother kept popping into my mind. It is only fitting that what I write here should also be dedicated to her.

Against all odds, she always followed these wise words, which I've always shared with my students, and I keep encouraging myself with today: YOU HAVE TO MAKE IT HAPPEN! Yes, she **DID** make it happen in so many ways! My wonderful mother, Mulvina Nykorchuk, had an exemplary teaching career (If I had only realized it more while I was growing up).

Apparently, her siblings were upset and even jealous that her parents sold the family cow in Saskatchewan so that they could afford to send her to teachers' college. When I was a child, my aunts told me how lucky she was and did not have to stay on the farm as they did. She was the oldest child and had two brothers and three sisters. It was not an easy life on the farm, to say the least. She walked six miles each day to school, even in the dead of winter. She witnessed terrible things, like my grandfather, whom I was told had a drinking problem, attempting to throw my grandmother down the well one day, and about that feeling of hopelessness. When my uncle came back from the war with PTSD, it seemed that the only medicine/treatment was alcohol back in those days. It was not surprising to learn that my very talented and artistic grandmother, Petrunia, who was also a wonderful cook (her deep-fried doughnuts were the best), had suffered a nervous breakdown and was institutionalized for some time during her life. She also lived with severe blindness for several years, and how she coped with that in those "dark" days is the stuff for another book. The garden scarecrows she created were admired by all.

My mom was my Grade One teacher, and I have only good memories of being in her class of 22 students. We were schooled in the living room of our home outside the city of Port Arthur, in the rural community of McIntyre Township, Ontario. Over the years, many of mom's students kept in contact with her after graduating and even visited her during their holidays, often bringing gifts, which were always proudly and prominently displayed in our home. When I began teaching, my mother gave me much guidance, advice, and assistance, along with many "tips and tidbits" that I still use to this day. She often went beyond the call of duty to help students.

I hope in some small way that this dedication to my mom helps me deal with the regret I still have in waiting too long to tell her how much I loved her, and what a good mother she was to me. Unfortunately, I spoke these heartfelt words to her while she was already suffering from advanced Alzheimer's disease, and confined to a facility where I visited her routinely most days after school. My mother died at age 84, November 2, (All Souls Day) 1999. To my great surprise, one of her former students, who apparently was living in a stressed home environment, found me on Facebook and wrote me an unbelievable letter of tribute to my mother, saying that she literally owes her life to her. She explained how my mom cared for her well-being, took charge, and she feels saved her life when she was so very ill and not well looked after. As a child, of course, I knew nothing of this. I just wish my mom could have read my book to see how much of what I learned from her is in it. Thank you, Mom!

Someone once said, **"If I turn into my mother or even half the woman she was, I'll consider my life a successful one."** That's how I feel too.

My book launch

Fundraising

Featured in S.T.E.M Magazine with my write up

Teaching a student

All dress for action

The love of living

She believed she could so she did

Suzy Tamasy

Suzy Tamasy is an entrepreneur, award-winning mentor in finance, and a leader in advocating for entrepreneurship as a way of creating positive transformation in the world. Suzy is the founder of *SuzyQJewels*, *Frugal Divas*, *Empowered in Heels*, *Biz & Fashion Magazine*, and *Women on Biz,* an initiative to radically transform how we support, celebrate and finance female entrepreneurs. She is also a blogger, event producer, and serial entrepreneur.

An entrepreneur and woman of style from an early age, Suzy understood from very early on that if she wanted something, she had to work for it, and it's that knowing that has helped her break the barriers and tenaciously pursue a love of fashion. Suzy started as a jewellery designer using recycled items and has evolved to her mini-empire with a virtual consignment shop and new clothing line under *SuzyQJewels & Frugal Divas*. Her clothing line donates a portion of its sales to women shelters across Ontario. Suzy also has two magazines – *Empowered in Heels* and *BF Biz & Fashion Magazine*.

To give back to the community, Suzy hosts a yearly Swap, Sell and Donate event and fashion show with her signature trademark walk showing the cycle of abuse and stopping the violence. Suzy strives to build relationships with her clients, encouraging them to never give up on their dreams because she believes that when we are open to the light of kindness, we can accomplish anything!

Suzy is currently based in Oshawa, Ontario with two lovely sons. Check out Suzy Q Jewels to learn more about the beauty, brains, and business-savvy of Suzy Tamasy.

https://www.facebook.com/empoweredinheels

Fundraising at Woodbridge Cruisers Fashion Show

Olimpia Tulpan

Olimpia Tulpan lives in Toronto Ontario but is originally from Romania. She is an entrepreneur who started by flipping condos in 2006, then went into decorating and Feng Shui. Olimpia's biggest passion is fashion, and everyone calls her a fashionista. She is also a published model and works in film. Olimpia was part of a series called *Empowered in Heels* by Suzy Tamasy, which is filmed in the studio of TV Chaar.

Olimpia became an advocate of a healthy lifestyle after her mother was diagnosed with cancer. In her journey to find a healthy and happy lifestyle, she became a reiki master and also does meditation in nature. When she's not working, Olimpia spends quality time with her friends who have become like family to her since she is alone in Canada.

www.Instagram.com/me_olimpia
https://www.facebook.com/olim.tulpan

Photographer JolVi Wedding Gown Suzyqjewels featured in Biz & Fashion Magazine

Cheryl Bailey

Cheryl Bailey is a photographer and artesian who resides in Durham Region, Ontario. She works primarily in oil-based pastels and ink on canvas. Cheryl specializes in lifestyle and wedding photography and recently added fashion photography to her repertoire.

Growing up in Toronto, Cheryl was surrounded by art. It was simply a way of life. One of her strongest influences, however, was her mother. Although her mother passed away when Cheryl was only 13 years old, she has always been able to feel her mom's positive energy around her. Cheryl believes the experiences she had growing up helped fuel her passion for helping people and ultimately catapulted her career into social work.

It's been her passion for photography though, that has truly enabled her to bridge those two worlds together. Cheryl has been shooting professionally since 1995. Her photographic style is fairly simple. It is modern, organic, and airy, but above all, honest. She strives to capture the real and the in-between moments that are unique to each situation and attempts to do so by creating a fun, energized, and candid environment during her photo sessions. For Cheryl, it's all about having a great time and being in the moment. When she's not behind the lens, Cheryl enjoys spending time with her husband, their son, and her two daughters.

https://www.facebook.com/CBPcherylbaileyphotography/
https://www.instagram.com/cherylbaileyphotography2019Mod

Model Em.T Photo Taken by Me

Demi Theo

Photographer Christine Lightbody working on Biz & Fashion Magazine Editorial

Demi Theo is a mother of two in Scarborough, Ontario. She is an interior designer, artist, writer, model, and show production co-organizer. After obtaining her bachelor of applied arts in Interior Design, she went on to design retail stores for an architectural firm. She started modelling in 2012 for a health and wellness company as their product ambassador and her photo is on one of their product boxes. She has written articles for many magazines, is a published model, and has participated in many runway shows and other events, as well as a music video.

One of Demi's dreams was to write and publish her very own children's book someday. This dream came true in the spring of 2021 when she became the author of a new children's book called *The Magical Chickadee and Friends - Stories and Crafts*, a project she completed before embarking on this wonderful journey with the co-authors of *Empowered in Heels*. When she is not busy organizing dance, fashion, and other related events, you can find Demi spending quality time with her family and friends. Demi enjoys the outdoors, movies, sports, crafting, music, gardening, and anything related to art.

"Never stop dreaming, never stop believing, never give up, neverstop trying and never stop learning." ~ Roy T. Bennett

https://www.instagram.com/demi.theo

265

Jennifer Traynor

Blissful Haze Photography

Jennifer Traynor is a wife, mother, and entrepreneur in Ajax, Ontario. She began teaching yoga part-time in 2019 and now also works as a virtual assistant. Pursuing both of these passions has allowed her to support other women while doing what she loves: yoga, meditation, mindfulness, writing, editing, designing, and creating.

Jennifer is a mental health advocate, as she has struggled with depression on and off for several years. She is open about her journey with mental health in the hopes that it not only helps to end the stigma but also serves as inspiration for others who struggle. Her experience with depression is ultimately what led her to the path she's on now. Her healing journey awakened a passion inside her to strive to help others, first through yoga and mindfulness, and then in supporting other female entrepreneurs.

Jennifer has had a life-long dream to become a published author. A graduate of the CentennialCollege print journalism program, she spent over 15 years working with major media outlets, being published as a blogger and copywriter before embarking on this journey with the co-authors of *Empowered in Heels*. The experience has sparked a drive in her to publish her own book and she has already begun a project to hopefully hit shelves in the near future.

When she's not busy in front of her laptop writing, editing, and content creation, you can find Jennifer spending quality time with her husband, Paul, their two children, Benjamin and Charlotte, and their dog, Seth. As a family, they are avid movie-watchers, enjoy epic family game nights, and love reading books together. On her own time, Jennifer likes to be in the company of good friends, practice yoga, or curl up on the couch to do word puzzles.

"The women whom I love and admire for their strength and grace did not get that way because sh*t worked out. They got that way because sh*t went wrong, and they handled it. They handled it in a thousand different ways on a thousand different days, but they handled it. Those women are my superheroes." ~ Elizabeth Gilbert
https://www.facebook.com/JenniferTraynorVA

https://www.instagram.com/jenn.traynor_va/

SHE is clothed in **STRENGTH** and **DIGNITY** and she **LAUGHS** without **FEAR** of the future

PROVERBS 31:25

Victoria Trinh

Victoria Trinh has been modelling and acting on and off since the age of four, although more seriously in the last 13 years her focus has been on modelling. She uses modelling as an artistic outlet to help deal with anxiety and depression. Victoria also finds modelling is a fun way to meet people, travel, and push her creative limits in fashion, projects, and shows. She was born and raised in Ontario, Canada, her background is Chinese and Vietnamese, and she speaks all three languages fairly well. Victoria likes to pull ideas from everyday inspirations and her dreams.

When she's not modelling you can find Victoria with her nose in a novel or her hands drawing and painting. She stays healthy with daily exercise and taking care of her mental health. You can learn more about Victoria on her social media.

https://www.instagram.com/vickymtrinh/

Sadia Salauddin

Originally of South Asian descent, Sadia Salauddin immigrated to Canada from Bangladesh in 1997 with her parents and sister. She started her university career at Ottawa University where she enrolled in the Business Administration program. She enjoyed her short time there but fell in love with the hustle and bustle of Toronto. She transferred her credits from the University of Ottawa and finished her Bachelor of Commerce degree at Ryerson University with a major in Marketing-Management and a minor in Communications.

Throughout her time in university, she received many modelling offers and started to enjoy exploring that side of her creative side.

Modelling has been a big hobby over the years and fashion is what she has embodied into not only her wardrobe but also her lifestyle. She has not only trained newcomers into the industry but also volunteered her time to help organize fashion shows. Humble yet highly ambitious, she has been seen on every major catwalk in Toronto and Mississauga. From Canadian Asian Fashion Week to modeling for some of the largest South Asian fashion designers in the world of Bollywood like Rohit K. Verma and Jaya Mishra.

Over the years, she has started to concentrate more on her full-time career and only gives time to unique and exclusive modeling offers. Apart from modelling, Sadia enjoys yoga, painting, swimming, music, movies, cooking, and spending time with her family and friends. She has hailed Toronto as her home for many years now and currently has a full-time career as the Assistant Director of Admissions at CDI College at their online division. Throughout this difficult era of Covid, she has gained strength from her faith and spirituality and claims that a close connection to God, yoga, friends, and family have kept her sane in what seems to be insane times.

https://www.instagram.com/sadia_sal

Kimberly Anne Cranley

Kimberly Anne Cranley is a mother of three beautiful girls and is happily married to her husband, Shaun, who works 12-hour shifts in the public sector. As busy as her family keeps her, she still has managed to find time to build a highly successful home-based business in the Health & Wellness industry working exclusively from her phone and on social media.

This dynamic and energetic woman entered into her very first Direct Sales company and hit the ground running only five years ago. After a trip to Orlando, Florida with four other women who were virtually strangers, she has hit rank after rank and helped women all over North America to find their purpose, gain back their health, and empower them to be and do anything they desire. Her team is devoted to her and together they are working towards building their empires.

Life wasn't always this blessed for this former young single mom who once lived on social assistance in low-income housing with her daughter. Kimberly has battled with depression and low self-confidence. Being an underdog all of her life, she now strives to show other women that no matter where they are in their lives and no matter what has happened in their past, they can still create the life they have always dreamed of.

"When you decide that going back is not an option, you'll find ways to grow into the person you were created to be. No change is easy but all growth is worthit. Burn every bridge in your life that causes you to settle for less." ~ Author Unknown

This is what Kimberly teaches her girls, and this is the passion from which her story is created. Her hope for those who read her story is to know that while she could have given up at any time, Kimberly had one driving force and that was a belief in something bigger than herself. She shares her story in the hopes that she may inspire others to continue pushing forward, no matter where they are right now or where they've come from.

https://www.kimberlycranley.com/

Beverley Thomson

Beverley was born in Ottawa and now resides in the Greater Toronto Area. Her mom was a born-again Christian and her dad was an inventor and wild man. She grew up with a mix of religion and how to party throughout her life. Beverley's mom passed away in 2013 as a minister in Guatemala helping children in need. Her father suffered a deep sadness and isolation from his alcoholism and took his own life in 2019.

Beverley left home in her early teens, wanting to see the world and live a life of passion instead of staying with her mom after her parents divorced. It wasn't as easy as she thought.

She had to work day and night to get herself through hairdressing school – but she did it! One day, a good-looking man came into the barbershop where she worked and swept her off her feet. They travelled the world together for nine years before she found out he was a cheater and involved in criminal activity. Beverley left him to start her life again. She went back to school and graduated with honours from college, becoming the only woman in her family to ever go further than high school. It was then she decided to go to university and get her Bachelors in Marketing and a Minor in Law so that one day she could support herself.

After working in the corporate world, she decided to open up her own cleaning business after a dream she had. Today she is a web designer, author, speaker, business owner, YouTuber, and free-spirited animal lover. Beverley's best achievement is trademarking and creating Maid Mart, a detailed residential and commercial cleaning company that covers the Greater Toronto Area. Her dream is to educate the public on the fair treatment of animals around the world. She has just finished working on her first of many children's books and is also a published poet. You can learn more about Beverley on her website: www.BeverleyThomson.com

"If you want to be successful, you have to jump, there's no way around it. When you jump, I can assure you that your parachute will not open right away. But if you do not jump, your parachute will never open. If you're safe, you'll never soar!" ~ Steve Harvey

Mackenzie Lubeck

Mackenzie Lubeck is 19 years old and was born and raised in St. Catharines, Ontario, Canada. From birth she always loved music and at two and a half years old was enrolled in dance lessons, starting with ballet. By the time Mackenzie was around five years old she started loving fashion and getting her photos taken. She was born into a family that was very close and supportive so that she could follow her dreams. Mackenzie always loved to make small plays, musicals, and fashion shows. When she was about 10 years old, she started drama classes with a local production company. This gave her many opportunities to participate in live theatre productions, which she loved doing for almost five years. During that time, she expanded her dance to jazz, tap, and lyrical. When she turned 16 years old, Mackenzie decided that she wanted to pursue her true dream of modelling. Her family arranged a professional photo shoot with a local photographer that included a makeup artist and hairdresser to see if she truly had a feel for it. She absolutely loved it and it was exactly what she dreamed of. Mackenzie had to put her dancing on hold so that she could concentrate completely on modelling, which she has now been doing for four years. She has also had the opportunity to walk in many runway shows, including New York Fashion Week. She loves the runway and that's where she comes to life.

Mackenzie loves travelling, whether it's for modelling or on family vacations. One of her favorite places to visit is the family cottage where she loves being on the water to go boating or fishing. She is also an excellent swimmer and had opportunities to swim competitively.

Mackenzie is a very compassionate person that has experienced a lot of bullying and cyberbullying in the past. For this reason, she is always trying to promote kindness and likes to build people up instead of tearing them down. She's a fun-loving girl who is always trying to make things better for someone else and loves to help others follow their dreams too. Mackenzie hopes to continue modelling and travelling in the future and has big goals ahead of her. During her spare time, you will find her writing poetry.

https://www.instagram.com/mckenzie.lubeck/

Me in Everday Clothing Photocredit Robert J. Deak Makeup Sara Leboudec

Sutha Shanmugarajah

Sutha Shanmugarajah graduated from the University of Toronto with a Bachelor of Science degree in Biochemistry. Currently, she works as a Clinical Research Coordinator for the Psoriatic Arthritis Program at the Toronto Western Hospital. She has a deep love of reading books with inspirational and motivational themes, as well as having a spiritual lifestyle.

Sutha spends her free time volunteering and assisting people in need.

She is dedicated to charity work and derives satisfaction from the happiness of those that she helps. Every year, Sutha takes part in different activities that bring meaning to her life.

In the past, she has done the United Way CN Tower Stair Climb, completed the 60km walk for the Weekend to End Breast Cancer, ran a half marathon to raise funds for arthritis, took part in multiple 5km/10km walks to raise funds for different charities, coordinated many bake sales to raise money for arthritis program, has coordinated food drives, and has helped prepare meals for the homeless in shelters. In addition, she has spearheaded a children's book drive and clothing drive that was devoted to impoverished families overseas. She takes on volunteer activities where there is a need for help. One of her meaningful volunteering opportunities was for the Invictus Games. Since last year, she has also been doing modelling and has been published many times. She has been on the cover of an international magazine, as well as has been interviewed by many media.

https://www.facebook.com/sutha.shanmugarajah.7/

https://www.instagram.com/sshanmug2019/

Pat Kozyra

Pat Kozyra (Nykorchuk) of Ukrainian descent was born, raised, and educated in Port Arthur (now ThunderBay), Ontario.

Twenty years ago, when she and her husband were "financially down and out," so to speak, because life had "thrown them lemons," Pat was experiencing panic, stress, depression, and desperation. Then, the expression she had always clung to and had tried to follow once again kicked in – these ten, simple, two-letter words: IF IT IS TO BE, IT IS UP TO ME! Fast forward to 2001 when she and her husband, Taras, left Canada to fulfill a two-year teaching contract in Hong Kong, which Pat was successful in obtaining, as a Learning Specialist for the Canadian International School of Hong Kong.

Now, twenty years later and back in Canada, as they both try to grasp the reality that those years have passed by so quickly and that the grandchildren can now drive cars and have jobs already, Pat and her husband are also getting used to life in retirement and presently live in Courtice, Ontario.

This seasoned professional, who is the mother of two daughters and the grandmother of six delightful grandchildren, has had an exemplary career. Pat has taught primary grades, Nursery, Pre-K, Kindergarten, vocal music, English as a second language, Gifted Education for 15 years, as well as being a Pre-school Coordinator, an Art Resource to teachers, and taught Special Education at Lakehead University. She is well known for her Webinar presentations and workshops for parents and teachers. Pat was the soloist for large Catholic churches in Thunder Bay, Toronto, and Hong Kong. She can be seen on her two YouTube channels called Read Me a Story and Hymns to Touch Your Heart. Yes, Pat has learned how to take lemons and make lemonade!

https://www.youtube.com/channel/UCc8RkJDGGKnVicBGn Ypt6_A

Touch Your Heart, St. Anne's Church, Stanley Hong Kong (Pat Kozyra and Peggie Fitch)
Streamed live on May 5, 2020

Paulus Waris Santoso

285

Amazing SQJ models and sisters we all have crown lets
Empower each other to shine!

A huge shout out to our supporter donation:

Gerry @gmiskophotography

G.Miako
Photography

JT John Taylor Models In Motion, , Stan Trac, Arshad Awan, Diana Winsor, Brenda Faulkner Mo Zee, Victor Ma, Mario Mule, Dale Mann, Cheryl Bailey, Shelley Ling Reid Marsala, Faisal Hafeez, Evangeline Cain, Daniel Schwartzberg, RB Johnathan Gill, Jenni M. Agudelo, TV Chaar, Olga Hutsul, Ralf Vandermeulen (In honour of your memory and support at all fundraising events) deceased 2021 and all the amazing models and make up artist I have had an opportunity to cross path with (the list is so abundant to put down)

So grateful to you all, Luv Suzy

Manufactured by Amazon.ca
Bolton, ON

27636936R00157